ENDLESS EVE

THE DAWN AT THE DUSK

NIHAL SRIVASTAV

Made with ♥ on the Notion Press Platform
www.notionpress.com

TO THE LIGHT THAT NEVER SHINES

TO THE FLOWER THAT NEVER BLOOMS

Contents

Acknowledgements

This journey through Endless Eve is deeply rooted in the transformative power of nature and the lessons learned from my own downfall. I am profoundly grateful to the natural world for its unwavering presence, reminding me of the cycles of life, loss, and renewal. The trees, the rivers, and the quiet moments in the wild have been my sanctuary, providing solace and inspiration during my darkest times.

To my own experiences of downfall, thank you for teaching me resilience. Through the depths of sorrow, I have discovered strength I never knew I had. It is through these struggles that I learned to embrace both pain and joy, finding beauty in the interplay between the two.

To all who read this book, may you find your own connection to the natural world and the strength that lies within your challenges. Thank you for embarking on this journey with me.

With deep appreciation

Foreword

In a world that often feels weighed down by sorrow, Endless Eve emerges as a poignant reminder of the resilience that lies within us all. This collection of poetry invites readers into the intimate journey of a boy navigating the labyrinth of grief, illuminating how profound loss can intertwine with the beauty of life's simplest moments.

As you read, you'll witness the delicate dance between despair and hope, as the boy grapples with his pain while discovering the transformative power of the present. This exploration is not just about loss; it is about the quiet strength that emerges when we allow ourselves to be vulnerable, and the unexpected joy that can arise even in the darkest of times.

In these pages, you will find reflections that resonate deeply, echoing the universal experience of longing, healing, and growth. Each poem serves as a stepping stone, guiding you through the shadows and into the light, reminding us that while grief may shape us, it does not define us.

It is my hope that Endless Eve inspires you to embrace your own journey— to find solace in the quiet moments, to seek joy amidst sorrow, and to recognize that every ending holds the promise of a new beginning.

Preface

In the twilight of sorrow and the dawn of renewal, Endless Eve unfolds a journey through grief and transformation. This poem invites you into the heart of a boy grappling with profound loss, only to discover solace in the simple joys of the present. As he navigates the shadows of his past and the brilliance of newfound hope, his story becomes a reflection on the resilience of the human spirit. Dive into Endless Eve and experience how even the deepest grief can lead to the most unexpected and beautiful revelations.

Prologue

In the hushed moments between dusk and dawn, when shadows linger and hope flickers like a candle in the dark, a boy stands at the edge of his own heartache. The world around him is heavy with memories, each one a weight that tugs at his spirit, pulling him deeper into a twilight of sorrow. Yet, amid the desolation, a whisper of renewal stirs—a fragile reminder that even the longest night must yield to the light.

As he grapples with the void left by loss, the boy embarks on a journey that leads him through the labyrinth of his grief. With each step, he encounters echoes of laughter and glimpses of beauty that intertwine with his pain, guiding him toward the simple joys that await in the present. Through the delicate interplay of shadow and light, he learns that transformation is born from acceptance, and that healing can blossom in the most unexpected of places.

In Endless Eve, the boy's story unfolds—a testament to the resilience of the human spirit. Here, grief is not merely an end, but a passage, and within its depths lies the potential for discovery. As you turn these pages, may you find solace in the understanding that even in our darkest moments, there exists the possibility of renewal, waiting to illuminate the path ahead.

1. Dusk's Embrace

The dusk whispers, in voices faint,
Of what was lost, a soft lament.
Like fingers of mist, it curls and winds,
Drawing him closer, where silence binds.
Each step is heavy, the air thick and cold,
Yet in the dark, he feels a hold.
Not of warmth, nor joy, nor light,
But of a calm that haunts the night.
The sky bruises, fading to black,
No stars to guide, no way back.
His hands tremble, reaching out wide,
But find only shadows by his side.
And still, he walks through time unbound,
With each breath, the weight grows profound.
The dusk pulls tighter, a lover's embrace,
Yet offers no solace, no saving grace.
In the hollow quiet, he listens close,
For echoes of what he needs the most.
But the voices are lost in a storm of haze,
Where memory and sorrow interlace.
His heart, once steady, beats in dismay,
Longing for a glimpse of day.

But the dusk holds him in its palm,
An endless night without a calm.
Beneath his feet, the earth feels thin,
A fragile line, where dusk begins.
It stretches onward, a threadbare road,
Carrying the weight of a heavy load.
Each step he takes seems carved in stone,
A march through shadows, cold and alone.
Yet somewhere, deep, a flicker stirs,
A distant memory that still recurs.
Once, the air was soft with bloom,
Not filled with echoes of this gloom.
Once, the sky was wide and bright,
Not drowned beneath this endless night.
He sees it there, beyond his reach,
A memory lost upon the beach,
Where waves of time have swept away,
All the remnants of the day.
And so, he walks, without a sound,
Through a world where grief is crowned.
The dusk, it shifts, a living thing,
A silent choir that does not sing.
Its arms surround him, a weightless chain,
Binding him to both loss and pain.
Yet, in its touch, he feels a thread,
Not of life, but what lies ahead.
For though the dusk is endless, still,

There is a peak beyond the hill.
A place where light, though faint, resides,
Beyond the reach of sorrow's tides.
It whispers, faint, beyond the dusk,
A promise made, a fragile trust.
Though shadows pull, though hope seems frail,
He feels the urge to lift the veil.
In the silence, in the dark,
A small, persistent, glowing spark.
Not yet a flame, but still it breathes,
A single thread within the leaves.
And so, he pauses, stands his ground,
Amidst the dark, where grief is found.
He wonders if the dusk will break,
And if the light is his to take.
In the silence, in the dark,
A small, persistent, glowing spark.
Not yet a flame, but still it breathes,
A single thread within the leaves.
And so, he pauses, stands his ground,
Amidst the dark, where grief is found.
He wonders if the dusk will break,
And if the light is his to take.
Yet still, the dusk pulls at his skin,
A tide of shadows, drawing him in.
It speaks in whispers, soft and low,
Of the comfort only it can bestow.

"Why chase the light," the shadows sigh,
"When in the dark, you learn to fly?"
And for a moment, he feels the truth,
In the cold embrace of forgotten youth.
The dusk, it knows his heart too well,
It carries secrets, it weaves a spell.
Each step he takes is bound by thread,
Of memories he thought long dead.
A voice, once golden, now faint as air,
Calls to him from everywhere.
Yet every time he turns his head,
He finds the voice was never said.
And so he walks, lost in between,
A world of shadows and unseen dreams.
The dusk grows heavy, thick as stone,
A cloak of night, all alone.
Yet through the fog, a glimmer gleams,
A crack of light within his dreams.
It calls to him, faint but bright,
A distant echo of the light.
He reaches out, but it fades away,
Like morning dew at the break of day.
His fingers grasp the empty air,
Nothing to hold, nothing there.
And still, he yearns, he cannot stop,
The hope that lingers, a rising drop.
For though the dusk holds tight its grip,

His heart still beats with a fragile skip.
And in the depths of the growing night,
He feels again the pull of light.
A memory, a distant shore,
Where he stood in the sun once more.
The warmth, the laughter, the tender breeze,
The sound of rustling in the trees.
It feels so close, he can almost taste,
The sweetness of a world embraced.
But as he reaches, the dusk pulls tight,
Reminds him it holds the endless night.
It whispers in his ear again,
Of the weight of loss, the cost of men.
"Why seek the day?" it softly croons,
"When you belong to these darkened moons?"
And though his soul trembles at its voice,
He knows deep down he still has choice.
For somewhere, hidden in the dusk,
Is a light he must trust.
It flickers faint, a distant call,
A fragile hope that may yet fall.
But still he steps, though shadows loom,
Through corridors thick with gloom.
Each step he takes, though slow, unsure,
Carries him closer to what is pure.
The path before him twists and bends,
A labyrinth that never ends.

Yet he walks, for to stand still,
Is to surrender to the chill.
And so he moves, his eyes ahead,
Searching for where the path is led.
The dusk surrounds him, a heavy shroud,
But he walks on, through the cloud.
The air is thick, the sky is dim,
But still, that flicker calls to him.
A star that hides behind the night,
A beacon of some forgotten light.
His feet are weary, his body aches,
But the hope within him never breaks.
For though the dusk is all he sees,
He knows the dawn waits in the trees.
The night is long, and shadows cling,
But deep within, he hears a ring.
A sound, a song, a distant hum,
That calls him toward the rising sun.
And so he walks, through fields of grey,
With eyes that search for a brighter day.
For though the dusk may seem to last,
He knows it's only shadows cast.
The light is there, beyond the veil,
A soft and tender, glowing trail.
It leads him on, though faint and slow,
Through the fields of long ago.
The dusk is thick, but he won't fall,

For somewhere, there awaits a call.
A voice, a hand, a golden light,
To guide him through the endless night.
And in the darkness, deep and true,
He feels the faintest hint of blue.
A sky that waits, just out of reach,
Beyond the shadows on the beach.
The tide rolls in, the waves are cold,
But still, he walks, still bold.
For though the night may hold him tight,
He knows there waits the coming light.
Each step is hard, the path unsure,
But he walks on, for he is sure.
The dusk will break, the night will end,
And in the light, he'll find a friend.
A hand to hold, a voice to hear,
A warmth to chase away the fear.
For though the dusk is long and wide,
It cannot last, it must subside.
And so he walks, though slow, though weak,
For it is the light he seeks.
The dusk, it pulls, it wraps, it winds,
But he walks on, for light he finds.
It glows, it calls, it leads him true,
Through fields of grey and skies of blue.
And in the end, the dusk will break,
And he'll be free, for light's own sake.

2. The void within

In the hollow night, where silence reigns,
He feels the pulse of lingering pains.
Each heartbeat echoes through empty space,
A hollow drum in a darkened place.
The morning's light, now stark and pale,
Cannot pierce through the sorrow's veil.
Each sunrise mocks with its golden hue,
As he stands lost, unsure and askew.
The day, once bright with hope and cheer,
Now stretches on, cold and austere.
He watches the sun climb the sky,
But its warmth no longer makes him sigh.
It's distant, faint, a ghostly glow,
A light that no longer seems to know
The path to reach his weary heart,
Which once danced with joy but now falls apart.
He roams the halls of memory's keep,
Where shadows of the past still creep.
Faces of those who've come and gone,
Haunt his steps, dusk till dawn.
Their laughter, once bright, now fades to grey,
Echoes of a time long slipped away.

He reaches for them, but they dissolve,
Like mist that time can never resolve.
Yet in this void, he seeks a way,
To find the dawn, to greet the day.
But every path seems cold and dark,
Each step a stumble, missing the mark.
He falters in the labyrinth of night,
Where shadows snuff out every light.
His heart, a compass lost in the storm,
Cannot remember the way to warm.
The weight of grief, a heavy shroud,
Hangs over him, dark and loud.
It presses down, a crushing weight,
Twisting his soul, sealing his fate.
And though he tries to push ahead,
The shadows whisper, filling him with dread.
They pull him back, they clutch his hands,
Leading him to barren lands.
The echoes of laughter now turned to sighs,
As he gazes at the empty skies.
The stars, once bright with endless dreams,
Now flicker like dying beams.
He tries to grasp the fleeting light,
That dances just beyond his sight.
But shadows tug at his weary soul,
As he struggles to regain control.
Each breath he takes feels like a chore,

The world outside, a distant shore.
He sees the colors drain away,
Leaving him trapped in endless grey.
The nights are long, the days are cold,
The joy he knew seems to have sold.
His soul, once vibrant, now feels numb,
As if the dawn may never come.
He wanders through his mind's terrain,
Seeking solace, battling pain.
His thoughts are echoes, drifting wide,
Caught in the flow of sorrow's tide.
Memories flicker, half-formed and faint,
Each one a brushstroke of the saint.
But they fade, they blur, they drift away,
Leaving him lost, unsure of the way.
He clings to fragments, lost and torn,
As the fabric of his hope is worn.
The void within is vast and deep,
Where shadows of the past silently creep.
They whisper truths he cannot deny,
That all he loved has said goodbye.
And yet he fights, though weak and spent,
Against the weight of his lament.
He fights against the tide of night,
Seeking dawn's forgiving light.
Yet hope persists, a distant call,
Amidst the darkness, faint but tall.

A voice within, a thread of grace,
That urges him to find his place.
It pulls him up when he would fall,
A fragile strength, though small, still tall.
He yearns for strength to see him through,
To find a path, to start anew.
The shadows press, they hold him tight,
But deep within, there burns a light.
It flickers, yes, but does not fade,
A tiny ember hope has made.
And in the darkness, faint but true,
He knows that he must push on through.
In the quiet, he makes a vow,
To face the shadows, to find his how.
The void may hold him in its grip,
But he will not let his courage slip.
He breathes in deep, he stands up tall,
Prepared to face the coming fall.
For though the path is long and steep,
It's through the void his soul must leap.
He steps ahead, though fear remains,
Though doubt and grief course through his veins.
He knows the light lies far beyond,
Past the night, where the shadows bond.
And though the void may call him back,
He walks on through the endless black.
For in his heart, there burns a flame,

That tells him he is not the same.
The night is long, but dawn will rise,
A sliver of hope in the empty skies.
He fights for it, he holds it near,
For it is the light that draws him clear.
The void may haunt, it may consume,
But in the end, the dawn will bloom.
And in that light, so far away,
He'll find the strength to greet the day.
The air is heavy, thick with strain,
As he walks through fields of pain.
His footsteps fall on barren ground,
A wasteland where no hope is found.
Each step is slow, a measured tread,
For fear the void will pull him dead.
Yet still he moves, though wearied so,
His heart determined not to slow.
The void within, it yawns so wide,
A chasm pulling him inside.
Its edges crumble, jagged, stark,
Threatening to consume the dark.
He feels its pull within his chest,
A hollow weight that steals his rest.
And yet, despite the endless fear,
He knows he cannot linger here.
For though the void calls out his name,
He senses something just the same—

A light, so distant, faint but true,
Beyond the night, beyond the blue.
It's there, somewhere, just out of reach,
A shore beyond the empty beach.
And though the waves of grief may rise,
He holds his gaze upon the skies.
His mind, it wanders through the past,
Through moments that were meant to last.
He sees their faces, hears their voice,
But all is faded, not by choice.
The echoes fade, the warmth subsides,
As shadows darken all his strides.
He reaches for them, but they flee,
Leaving him adrift at sea.
Yet still he fights, though weak and worn,
Through nights so long and days forlorn.
He feels the void pulling him down,
But something deeper makes him frown.
For in the darkness, cold and bleak,
There lies a whisper, faint and weak.
It calls him from the depth of night,
A whisper of the distant light.
He knows the void would swallow whole,
The fragments left within his soul.
It offers silence, deep and sure,
A promise that it will endure.
And yet, he finds he cannot bend,

For though the void seems like a friend,
It offers nothing but despair,
A hollow world without a care.
The night is thick, the stars are faint,
Each one a fading, distant saint.
They call to him, though far away,
To seek the light, to find the day.
But every time he takes a step,
The void pulls tight, a final rep.
It wants to claim his heart for good,
To take him where no other could.
And so, he walks, unsure and frail,
Through endless night and sorrow's wail.
His heart is heavy, full of grief,
But still he seeks some small relief.
He knows the light is distant still,
But something deep within his will
Refuses now to give in fast,
For he knows this night cannot last.
In the silence, he hears a sound,
A soft and gentle, distant bound.
It echoes through the hollow air,
A song of hope, a song so rare.
It hums and sways within the night,
A melody of faint delight.
And though he cannot see its source,
He feels it guide him, like a course.

The void, it presses hard and tight,
But in his heart, there stirs a light.
A flicker, small but strong enough,
To help him rise, though times are tough.
For in the dark, he feels a breeze,
A breath of air, a touch of ease.
And though the shadows still hold sway,
He knows that there will come a day.
The weight of grief is not yet gone,
The fight is long, the road is drawn.
But every step, though slow, unsure,
Brings him closer to something pure.
The void, it roars, it threatens all,
But deep inside, he stands up tall.
For though the darkness holds him tight,
He knows that somewhere waits the light.
His mind is clouded, thick with doubt,
But something stirs, something about
The way the stars still try to shine,
Gives him a hope, a fragile line.
And so, he walks, though slow and weak,
Through the night, to find what he seeks.
For in the void, there lies a spark,
A sliver of light within the dark.
He feels the void recede, withdraw,
Its grip no longer filled with awe.
For though it holds him in its grasp,

He feels his heart begin to clasp
The thought of something just ahead,
Beyond the shadows, past the dread.
It's faint, but there, a gentle glow,
A light that only he can know.
And so he walks, though shadows fall,
He holds within a hope so small.
It leads him on, through endless night,
A flicker of some distant light.
And though the void still holds him near,
He feels a strength, though not so clear.
For in his heart, a truth takes root,
That darkness cannot follow suit.
The void, though vast and full of pain,
Cannot drown out the morning's gain.
For though the night is long and deep,
The dawn will come, it will not keep.
And he, though weak and full of fear,
Will rise again, will persevere.
For in the dark, there is a way,
To find the light, to greet the day.
He stands within the hollow night,
And though he trembles, he holds tight.
The void, it calls, it wants him still,
But something deeper stirs his will.
For in the silence, there's a sound,
A song of hope, of peace unbound.

It echoes through the endless black,
A promise that there's no turning back.
The road ahead is long and steep,
The shadows thick, the void so deep.
But still, he walks, with fragile grace,
To find the dawn, to see its face.
For in the dark, he knows for sure,
That light will come, that he'll endure.
The void, it may surround him so,
But in his heart, the light will grow.

3. Shadows of the Past

In dreams he wanders, lost and cold,
Through fields of memories, bitter and old.
The laughter that once lit up his night,
Now flickers faint, a dying light.
He drifts through corridors of time,
Where echoes ring in a mournful chime.
Each step is heavy, laden with dread,
As shadows of the past weave around his head.
He clings to moments, fleeting and rare,
A touch, a glance, a whispered prayer.
But time, relentless, steals them away,
Leaving him stranded, led astray.
The hands of the clock move on too fast,
Erasing the moments that couldn't last.
And though he grasps at the fleeting hue,
The memories slip through, as if they knew.
The shadows deepen, growing long,
Each memory now feels wrong.
What once was sweet, now tastes of ash,
As he sifts through the broken cache.
He searches through the remnants of his days,
Through a world that now seems to haze.

The joy he once knew now feels remote,
Like a distant ship afloat.
Yet still, he reaches through the haze,
Seeking solace in the old ways.
But the past, a phantom, slips his grasp,
Leaving only a hollow clasp.
He tries to hold onto the warmth once near,
But it dissolves in the cold of fear.
Each touch, each word, each silent plea,
Now lost to a past that refuses to be.
He wanders through the hallways of yore,
Where echoes of laughter are no more.
The walls, once vibrant, now cracked and worn,
Bear witness to the soul's forlorn.
The colors have faded, the light has died,
Leaving him to wander, to seek and hide.
Each room, each corner, a place of grief,
A reminder of joy turned to thief.
Faces blur and voices fade,
The joyful scenes now starkly laid.
What was once clear is now a mist,
A memory that can no longer persist.
He sees their smiles, their gentle grace,
But they vanish before he can trace.
Each laughter, each shared embrace,
Now an echo in a desolate space.
He seeks the warmth of yesteryears,

But finds instead the cold of fears.
The past, once a beacon, now a mire,
Dragging him into its cold quagmire.
He searches for the comfort it once gave,
But the memories have become a grave.
Each moment that once was bright and clear,
Now obscured by the veil of fear.
The shadows of his past loom large,
As he struggles to regain his charge.
They tower over him, a darkened wall,
Threatening to make him fall.
Each shadow a reminder of what was lost,
Each one a symbol of the cost.
He grapples with them, tries to see,
The truth behind their mystery.
The past is a book with pages torn,
Each chapter a tale of joy now worn.
He reads the lines with tearful eyes,
Searching for a truth amidst the lies.
The ink is smudged, the words are faint,
Leaving him to question and taint.
He seeks a meaning in the fractured tales,
But only finds a series of failed trails.
The memories are ghosts of what once was,
Each one a shadow of the cause.
They drift through his mind, elusive and pale,
Leaving behind a haunting trail.

He tries to grasp what's left behind,
But finds it slipping through his mind.
Each ghost a reminder of the past,
A moment that could never last.
In the silence, he hears the cries,
Of moments lost, of fading ties.
The past speaks in a language of pain,
A constant echo, a lingering strain.
He listens for the voices he once knew,
But they are drowned by the darkness he grew.
Each cry a reminder of the cost,
Of the joy and warmth that was lost.
The past, a mirror to his soul,
Reflects the pain, the empty hole.
He sees his own face in its depths,
A shadow of the self he wept.
The reflection is distorted, unclear,
A reminder of the sorrow and fear.
He gazes into the mirror's crack,
Seeking a way to turn back.
Yet amidst the shadows, a glimmer shows,
A light that through the darkness grows.
It flickers softly, a distant ray,
Promising that dawn will find a way.
He reaches out, though hesitant, slow,
For the light that seems to gently glow.
It calls him forward, through the pain,

To seek the truth beyond the chain.
He hopes that in the depths of night,
He'll find the strength to seek the light.
The shadows may loom, the memories fade,
But he holds fast to the hope he's made.
For in the darkest hour, a light can shine,
And guide him through the pain, divine.
He takes a step towards the faintest gleam,
To escape the shadows of a forgotten dream.
And so he walks, through shadows cast,
Seeking redemption from his past.
Each step a journey through the pain,
To find the joy, to break the chain.
The path is long, the night is deep,
But he persists, though weary and weak.
For in the end, he knows the truth,
That he must seek to find his youth.
The shadows may darken, the past may wail,
But he will walk through, without fail.
For in the journey through the dark,
He will find the light, a hopeful spark.
Each memory, though lost and torn,
Is a guide through the night, a promise sworn.
He walks on, through the echoes and pain,
To find the joy, to break the chain.
He wanders through the remnants of time,
A realm where echoes softly chime.

The rooms are filled with silent screams,
Fragments of once cherished dreams.
Each door he opens, each corner turned,
Reveals a past for which he yearned.
Yet, the warmth he seeks is ever out of grasp,
Lost to the void, to shadows' clasp.
In the darkened corners of his mind,
He seeks the solace he cannot find.
The faces from his past appear in mist,
A fleeting vision, a whispered kiss.
They dance in the periphery of his sight,
A reminder of a long-lost light.
He reaches out with trembling hands,
But the apparitions slip through his strands.
He navigates the labyrinth of his soul,
Where memories twist, take their toll.
Each hallway is a mirror of regret,
Reflecting the past he can't forget.
The laughter that once filled his days,
Now echoes through a haunting haze.
The joy of moments shared and gone,
Is now a shadow on the lawn.
As he moves through the corridors of grief,
He clings to hope, seeks some relief.
Yet each room reveals a deeper pain,
Each sight a reminder of loss's chain.
He tries to decipher the cryptic clues,

To find the path that he can use.
But the shadows grow and intertwine,
Each one a testament to time.
The past, with its whispers and moans,
Weaves a web of mournful tones.
He walks the threads of what was lost,
Tracing each thread, no matter the cost.
In the silence, he hears the distant call,
Of memories that rise and fall.
They pull him back with a gentle might,
Threatening to engulf him in the night.
The faces he encounters are mere traces,
Fading into empty spaces.
Their voices are echoes in the wind,
Their warmth a memory grown thin.
He longs to hold onto their embrace,
To find their comfort in this place.
But they slip away, like sand through fingers,
Leaving only a pain that lingers.
Yet amidst the shadows, a light persists,
A beacon that through darkness twists.
It shines softly, a distant glow,
Guiding him through the sorrow's flow.
He follows it with weary stride,
Hoping it will turn the tide.
For though the past holds him tight,
The light may guide him to the night.

Each step he takes is heavy, slow,
Through the darkness, he must go.
The shadows press, the memories sting,
Yet he holds onto a distant string.
The hope that somewhere, beyond the pain,
There lies a joy that can remain.
He follows the light, though frail and thin,
Believing it will help him win.
He crosses thresholds into memories dim,
Each one a challenge, a requiem.
The halls are lined with relics of the past,
Each one a fragment that couldn't last.
He touches the walls, feels their cold,
And wonders how the joy grew old.
The warmth he once knew is now a trace,
A reminder of a distant place.
As he navigates through these haunted halls,
He listens to the silence that calls.
The void speaks in a language clear,
A reminder of the pain he holds dear.
But within the darkness, he feels a push,
A gentle nudge, a hopeful hush.
It whispers that redemption is near,
That light will break through the sphere.
The memories continue to twist and turn,
Each one a lesson he must learn.
The past may be a shadowy maze,

But he's determined to find the rays.
For in the depths of his despair,
He feels a strength, a guiding flare.
He knows that though the shadows loom,
The light will pierce through the gloom.
He treads on, through the past's embrace,
Facing the void with steadfast grace.
Each shadow a challenge, each memory a test,
To find the peace, to find the rest.
The journey is long, the night is deep,
But he persists, through tears and sleep.
For he believes that in the end,
The shadows will retreat, and light will mend.
In the silence of the night, he stands,
A warrior with trembling hands.
The past may haunt, the shadows may play,
But he is ready for a new day.
For within the shadows, he's found a spark,
A light that guides him through the dark.
He walks with purpose, through the pain,
To find the joy, to break the chain.
The memories may be ghosts of old,
But he holds onto the hope they hold.
Each step forward is a victory won,
A stride towards the rising sun.
And though the past still calls his name,
He will not falter, he will not wane.

For in the journey through the night,
He will find the strength to seek the light.
As he moves through the shadows vast,
He feels a shift, a break at last.
The darkness may have held him tight,
But the dawn will come with the light.
He perseveres through the echoes and fears,
Guided by hope through the years.
For in the depths of shadows cast,
He finds the promise of peace at last.

4. The mask we wears

By day, he dons a practiced smile,
A mask to hide the inner trial.
To those who ask, he simply replies,
With words well-rehearsed, crafted lies.
"I'm fine," he says, with a gentle nod,
As inside, his spirit's deeply flawed.
The mask is firm, no crack, no tear,
But beneath, the grief lays bare.
In the crowded streets, amidst the throng,
He walks in step, as though he belongs.
Yet every footfall feels like a weight,
A silent burden he cannot abate.
His laughter, though soft, seems real enough,
But it's just a way to hide the rough.
Inside, a storm rages on and on,
But he keeps it hidden, until it's gone.
Every smile is a well-placed stone,
In a fortress where he stands alone.
The world sees strength, a steady hand,
But they do not see the shifting sand.
Behind the calm of his practiced face,
Lies a heart that's lost in empty space.

He wears the mask like armor, strong,
Yet he wonders how long he can go along.
The mask serves its purpose, day by day,
Keeping the curious at bay.
He's mastered the art of seeming fine,
Of playing his part, toeing the line.
But at night, when the world is asleep,
The cracks in the mask begin to seep.
In the quiet, when no one can see,
He lets himself simply be.
He sits alone, in the dim-lit room,
Where shadows dance and the silence looms.
The mask, discarded, falls to the floor,
And the weight of it feels like a door—
A door to the pain he tries to deny,
To the sorrow that never seems to die.
He presses his hands to his face and sighs,
Releasing the tears he tries to hide.
The mask he wears is a perfect art,
Yet it doesn't shield his aching heart.
He knows too well the cost it bears,
The endless weight of hidden cares.
For every smile he gives away,
Another piece of him slips away.
The performance drains him, day by day,
But he keeps it up, come what may.
Behind the laughter, the lighthearted jest,

He's a man who's never at rest.
His mind churns with questions and fears,
His heart, heavy with uncried tears.
Yet to show the truth would be too much—
To expose the hurt, the fear, the clutch.
So, he hides it all behind the mask,
Performing well, as though it's a task.
In every conversation, every glance,
He performs the well-rehearsed dance.
A smile here, a nod there,
A casual word without a care.
But deep inside, the weight remains,
A silent scream, a constant strain.
He wishes someone could see through the veil,
To notice the cracks where he is frail.
But people are content with what they see—
The surface of him, not the deep sea.
They believe the mask without a doubt,
And never wonder what it's all about.
They don't see the nights when he's alone,
When the silence cuts right to the bone.
They don't hear the sobs he stifles down,
Or see him as he begins to drown.
There are moments when he wonders why—
Why he keeps up the endless lie.
Why he pretends to be alright,
When inside, he's losing the fight.

But the mask is easier than the truth,
Easier than revealing the ruthless
Reality that he's been hiding for years,
That behind the mask, there's only fears.
The mask has become a part of him now,
A shield he doesn't know how
To remove, even if he wanted to,
For it has become his point of view.
The mask is him, and he is the mask,
Both intertwined in the same task.
And though he dreams of setting it down,
He doesn't know if he'd survive the crown.
For the world expects him to be strong,
To carry on, to go along.
He can't let them see the cracks beneath,
The endless grief, the lack of belief.
So, he carries on, day by day,
Hiding the pain, come what may.
But in his heart, he knows the cost—
That he's losing himself, he's already lost.
At night, when he's alone in bed,
The mask is gone, the grief instead
Comes pouring forth, a tidal wave,
And he wonders if he can be saved.
He buries his face in trembling hands,
Trying to understand
Why the mask has become his way,

And whether he'll ever see a day
Where he doesn't need to wear it anymore,
Where he can be himself once more.
He dreams of a time when he'll be free,
When the mask will no longer be
A part of him, a second skin,
When he'll let the light back in.
But for now, he wears it still,
A protector, against his will.
For though it shields him from the world's gaze,
It also traps him in a maze.
The mask hides his pain from view,
But it keeps him from being true.
He longs to scream, to tear it apart,
To show the world his aching heart.
But he fears what they would say,
How they would look at him that way.
So, he keeps it on, tight and secure,
Hoping someday he'll find a cure.
Perhaps there's a light beyond the veil,
A place where he won't have to trail
Behind the mask, hidden and cold,
A place where he can be bold.
But for now, he wears it still,
A shield, a burden, an iron will.
He smiles and nods, plays his part,
Hiding the truth within his heart.

And as the days go by, one by one,

He hopes for the rising sun—

A time when he won't have to pretend,

When the mask can finally end.

But until that day comes, he'll carry on,

Wearing the mask from dusk till dawn.

For it's all he knows, all he can bear,

A way to hide, a way to care.

The mask is a prison of his own design,

A shield, a cage—both intertwined.

He crafted it in times of need,

When he couldn't let himself bleed.

But now it's all he's ever known,

A wall between him and the unknown.

Each morning he wakes, he puts it on,

A ritual, an unspoken song.

It's second nature now, to hide,

To push the pain and fear aside.

He longs to tear the mask away,

To show the world the shades of gray

That color his thoughts, his every dream,

But it's harder than it might seem.

The mask is safety, it keeps him whole,

Even as it takes a toll

On his soul, his fragile heart—

A defense, yet tearing him apart.

He recalls the times before it came,

Before he felt the need to tame
His emotions, raw and true,
Before the world saw him askew.
Back when he could laugh without a care,
When his face was bare, his spirit rare.
But that was a lifetime ago,
A time before the cracks could show.
Now the mask is all he wears,
A refuge from the world's glares.
He's forgotten how it feels to be
Unmasked, open, and truly free.
The burden of the mask is clear,
But the alternative, he fears, is near—
The thought of showing what's inside,
The fear, the grief, the endless tide.
There are moments when he almost tries,
When the mask begins to slip, and he cries
Out for help, for someone to see,
But the fear of judgment won't let him be.
He pulls the mask tighter, seals the cracks,
And once again, he turns his back
On the world, on the chance to heal,
For the mask feels safer, more real.
The longer he wears it, the more it weighs,
Dragging him down through endless days.
Yet still, he keeps it on, afraid—
Afraid of the life he might have made

Without it, if only he had been strong,
If only he hadn't gone along
With the act, the charade, the game,
Hiding his truth in layers of shame.
Every time he looks in the mirror,
The reflection grows a little clearer.
He sees the cracks, the lines of strain,
The weight of years of silent pain.
The mask is strong, but it's wearing thin,
And he fears the darkness creeping in.
How long can he keep it up, he wonders,
Before the weight pulls him under?
In those rare, quiet moments of thought,
He dreams of tearing the mask he's wrought.
What would it be like to be seen,
To show the world where he's truly been?
To let them witness all he hides,
The fears, the hopes, the crashing tides?
But then, the doubt returns in force—
What if they turn away, of course?
What if they see him, bare and true,
And reject the person they never knew?
The mask protects him from that fate,
A barrier between love and hate.
It keeps the world at arm's length,
Even as it drains his strength.
It allows him to survive the day,

But at night, it begins to fray.
In the darkness, when all is still,
He confronts the void, the growing chill.
The mask slips off, revealing all—
The endless void, the silent call.
Without it, he feels so weak,
So vulnerable, unable to speak.
The mask may be a burden, a weight,
But without it, he fears his fate.
He's tried before to set it down,
To free himself from its heavy crown.
But each time, the fear returns anew,
Reminding him of what he'll lose.
The mask is safe, the mask is sure,
It shields him from a world unsure.
Without it, he's exposed, he's raw,
Vulnerable to every flaw.
The mask hides not just his pain,
But the shame, the guilt, the strain
Of a life lived in shadows deep,
A life where secrets never sleep.
The mask allows him to pretend,
To present a face that doesn't bend.
But beneath, the truth is stark and cold,
A life lived half, never bold.
He dreams of days when he'll be free,
When the mask will no longer be

A part of him, a second skin,
When he can let the light back in.
But for now, it shields him well,
A defense against the personal hell
That waits to swallow him whole,
To drag him into the darkest hole.
Yet, as the days grow longer still,
He feels the mask slipping, against his will.
It's wearing thin, fraying at the seams,
And he's haunted by restless dreams.
What happens when the mask gives way?
Will he finally face the light of day?
Or will he crumble, fall apart,
Too fragile to mend his broken heart?
The mask is his companion, sure,
But even he knows it's not the cure.
It keeps him safe, but at a cost,
For behind it, much is lost.
The person he could have been,
The joy, the hope, the love within.
The mask may shield him from the pain,
But it also keeps him bound in chains.
And yet, he wonders, every night,
What it would be like to fight—
To cast the mask aside and stand
Bare and open, hand in hand
With his grief, his sorrow, his fear,

To show the world what's hidden here.
To take the risk, to face the unknown,
To finally feel he's not alone.
But the fear remains, a constant guide,
A whisper that he can't abide.
The mask is safety, the mask is peace,
It offers a small, if bitter, release.
He knows it's not forever—no,
One day, he'll have to let it go.
But for now, he wears it still,
A shield, a burden, against his will.
The mask he wears, a fragile guise,
Conceals the pain behind his eyes.
But in his heart, he knows the truth—
That one day soon, he'll have to choose.
To live behind the mask forevermore,
Or take it off and find the door
To a life where he can be real,
Where he can show the world how he feels.
And so, he waits, caught in between,
A world of masks, a world unseen.
He hopes for courage, hopes for grace,
To one day show his true face.
For now, the mask is his disguise,
But in his heart, the future lies—
A future where he's free at last,
No longer hiding from his past.

5. Whispers in the Wind

One day, in the park, he hears a sound,
A gentle whisper, soft and profound.
The wind it seems, carries a song,
A melody where he might belong.
The leaves rustle with a quiet grace,
Bringing a smile to his weary face.
The sound is faint, a distant hum,
Yet it beckons him to overcome.
He follows the whisper through the trees,
Where sunlight dances with the breeze.
Each step he takes, a step away,
From the shadows where he used to stay.
In this place, so pure, so bright,
He feels the stirrings of new light.
The wind, a guide, so calm, so clear,
Whispers softly, "There's nothing to fear."
The rustling leaves, a soothing song,
Carry him where he feels he belongs.
Each whisper seems to call his name,
Guiding him from the dark's cruel game.
He breathes in deeply, fills his soul,
With hope and dreams that start to roll.

The wind, a balm for his aching heart,
Brings a chance for a brand new start.
The path before him is overgrown,
But with each step, he feels less alone.
The whispers lead him to a place,
Where shadows fade, replaced by grace.
He reaches out to touch the breeze,
Feeling the comfort it bestows with ease.
In the whispers, he finds a friend,
A promise that the dark will end.
Yet still, the shadows lurk behind,
Ghosts of the past he cannot unwind.
Their whispers too, though faint and weak,
Echo with truths he dares not speak.
They tug at him, pull at his sleeve,
Reminders of all he had to leave.
But here, amidst the wind's soft sigh,
He feels a peace, though he knows not why.
He sits beneath a towering tree,
And lets the wind flow wild and free.
It carries with it scents of earth,
Of life renewed, of quiet rebirth.
The breeze, so gentle, caresses his skin,
Stirring the strength he holds within.
In the rustling grass, in the sway of the leaves,
He begins to believe, begins to believe.
The sky above, so vast, so blue,

A reminder that hope is not yet through.
The sun breaks through the canopy's shade,
And in its warmth, his fears begin to fade.
For years, he wandered, lost in night,
But now he walks toward the light.
And though the shadows still remain,
The wind whispers of release from pain.
His footsteps fall with quiet grace,
As though the earth embraces his pace.
The birds call out, their songs so clear,
A melody that calms his fear.
The world around him seems alive,
Urging his tired soul to strive.
For too long, he's hidden in the dark,
But now he feels the smallest spark.
He walks further, through the winding path,
And listens close to the wind's soft laugh.
It dances around him, light and free,
Whispering secrets only he can see.
The world, so vast, so full of light,
Seems to welcome him from endless night.
Each breeze, each gust, each stirring air,
Carries whispers that lead him to care.
In the distance, the trees begin to part,
Revealing a meadow, pure of heart.
The grass is tall, the flowers in bloom,
And in the air, no sense of gloom.

He steps into this place so wide,
And lets the wind be his only guide.
For in this space, so pure, so bright,
He feels the stirrings of renewed light.
The whispers now, so soft, so kind,
Speak to the depths of his troubled mind.
They tell him stories of days to come,
Of joy, of peace, of battles won.
They weave a tapestry of hope and dreams,
Of paths untaken, flowing streams.
And though his heart still holds its scars,
He feels the pull of distant stars.
He closes his eyes and breathes it in,
The wind, the earth, the softening din.
He feels the presence near at hand,
Guiding him through this unknown land.
It is a force he cannot see,
Yet feels it watching, silently.
And in that presence, he finds a way,
To keep the darkness at bay.
The park becomes his sacred space,
A place where shadows lose their trace.
He returns each day, to walk the trail,
To feel the wind, so soft and frail.
And with each visit, he feels more whole,
As if the whispers soothe his soul.
They guide him through the pain and strife,

Toward the light, toward a new life.
Yet not all days are clear and bright,
For still, the darkness holds its fight.
There are times the shadows pull him down,
And he drowns beneath their heavy crown.
The whispers fade, the wind grows still,
And all he feels is a chilling thrill.
But even in these darkest hours,
The memory of the wind empowers.
He recalls the way it spoke his name,
How it carried him through the shame.
And even when the night is long,
He remembers the wind's soft song.
It sings of hope, of light to come,
Of battles fought and battles won.
And though the shadows grasp his heart,
He knows he will not fall apart.
For deep within, a flame still burns,
A light that never truly turns.
It flickers faint, but does not die,
And in its glow, he sees the sky.
The wind, the trees, the world so wide,
All beckon him to step inside.
To leave the darkness, cold and grim,
And let the light flow deep within.
So once again, he walks the trail,
And lets the wind's soft voice prevail.

It whispers still, so calm, so clear,
"There's nothing left for you to fear."
He breathes in deeply, fills his lungs,
And feels the song that's just begun.
For though the shadows still remain,
He knows the wind will soothe his pain.
The park, now bathed in golden light,
Becomes his refuge, pure and bright.
And in its whispers, soft and kind,
He leaves the darkened past behind.
Each step he takes, a step toward grace,
A step away from that dark place.
And though the path is still unknown,
He knows he no longer walks alone.
The wind, once a gentle guide, grows bold,
As if it carries stories untold.
It swirls around him, lifting his hair,
Filling the air with a quiet prayer.
There's magic here, he cannot deny,
In the rustling trees and the open sky.
The world seems larger than before,
Each whisper unlocking a hidden door.
He pauses now, beneath a tree,
Its ancient limbs sway wild and free.
The wind dances in the branches above,
Whispering secrets of life and love.
He reaches out, fingers splayed wide,

As if to touch the breath of the tide.
The air wraps around him, warm and bright,
And for the first time, he feels the light.
It's not just the sun that pierces his heart,
But something deeper, a healing start.
The whispers, though soft, carry weight,
Speaking of things beyond mere fate.
They tell of roads not yet tread,
Of life that continues, even when fled.
He listens closely, straining to hear,
The voice that calls, so faint yet near.
The wind speaks now with a firmer tone,
Reminding him he's never alone.
It beckons him forward, urging him on,
Toward a place where the shadows are gone.
The path ahead is winding and steep,
But it's one he knows he must keep.
For though the darkness still clings to his side,
The wind pushes him, acting as his guide.
He takes another step, then one more,
Feeling the weight he carried before,
Begin to lift, begin to fade,
As the whispers lead him through the glade.
He walks now with purpose, slow but sure,
Knowing that healing is not a cure,
But a journey, a winding road,
Where light and darkness share the load.

The park, once a mere escape,
Has become a place where dreams take shape.
Each tree, each flower, each blade of grass,
Feels like a portal to the past.
But this time, the past does not bind,
It's a part of him, but no longer confined.
He lets the memories come and go,
Like the wind that continues to flow.
And in the wind, he hears the past,
Not as a weight, but as something vast.
It no longer haunts him with cruel intent,
But speaks of moments, well-lived, well-spent.
The laughter, the love, the pain, the tears,
All the memories, now softened by years.
They swirl around him, but do not sting,
Instead, they make his tired heart sing.
The whispers change, taking on new form,
They speak of resilience, of weathering the storm.
They tell him he's stronger than he knows,
That even in darkness, a seed still grows.
The wind, his constant companion now,
Pushes him onward, showing him how.
It guides his steps, one by one,
Toward a future where he's not undone.
The meadow opens wide before his eyes,
A sea of green beneath blue skies.
The wind, like a painter, strokes the scene,

With golden light and shadows serene.
He stands at the edge, heart in his throat,
As the whispers shift to a higher note.
The wind seems to sing, a melody pure,
Telling him that there is still more to endure.
But with that endurance comes great reward,
A life rebuilt, a spirit restored.
He steps into the meadow, feeling the earth,
Alive with promise, with endless rebirth.
The whispers swirl around his feet,
As if guiding him toward something sweet.
He follows their lead, trusting their call,
Knowing that he can rise after the fall.
The past, now a shadow, lingers behind,
But it no longer controls his mind.
The whispers remind him, time and again,
That he's walking forward, leaving the pain.
He breathes in deeply, filling his lungs,
With air that's alive with songs unsung.
The wind lifts him, carries him high,
Toward a place where the soul can fly.
He feels the presence near once more,
A guiding force, strong to the core.
It's as if the wind itself is alive,
Helping him, urging him to strive.
He closes his eyes, lets it take him there,
To a world where the air is light and fair.

And in that moment, he feels the grace,
Of something far beyond time and space.
The wind whispers softly in his ear,
"There's nothing left for you to fear."
The shadows retreat, the light floods in,
And he knows now, the healing will begin.
For though the journey is far from complete,
He's found a place where the soul can meet,
The whispers of hope, the voice of the wind,
That tells him his life is not at its end.
He stays in the meadow, long and still,
Letting the wind fill him at will.
Each gust, each breath, a reminder clear,
That even in sorrow, there's hope to steer.
The park, his sanctuary, his sacred place,
Where he found solace, where he found grace.
And in the whispers, soft and true,
He discovered the strength to start anew.
As the day fades, and the sky turns gold,
He feels a peace, gentle and bold.
The wind quiets, the whispers cease,
Leaving behind a sense of peace.
He stands there, alone but whole,
Finally feeling the quiet of his soul.
The whispers, though gone, have left their mark,
Guiding him through the endless dark.
And though the night may come once more,

He knows he's stronger than before.
For the wind has shown him, time and again,
That light will return, even after the rain.
The whispers will always be there to guide,
No matter how dark the shadows might hide.
And with that knowledge, he walks away,
Toward the dawn of a brand new day.

6. The Children's Laughter

In the park, where shadows once lay,
He wanders through the fading gray.
The air is crisp with autumn's breath,
A stark contrast to his lingering death.
Among the trees, where light breaks through,
He hears a sound both fresh and new.
A laughter, light, and full of cheer,
Cuts through the silence, sharp and clear.
He stands in stillness, heart a cage,
While echoes of the past rage.
The children's voices, bright and true,
Speak of a world he once knew.
Their games are wild, their joy immense,
Each laugh a beacon, an innocence.
From a distance, he observes their play,
A vibrant dance in the fading day.
Their feet kick up the fallen leaves,
A playful swirl that gently weaves.
The sun above, a golden dome,
Illuminates their frolic, their home.

In the quiet, his heart begins to stir,
A warmth, a flicker, a gentle purr.
Each giggle, each shout, a soothing balm,
Turning his sorrow into calm.
Yet, he hesitates, the shadows near,
Fearing the joy that draws him clear.
His mind wrestles with doubt and fear,
Is he deserving of this cheer?
Can he, a soul so marred by pain,
Find solace in such pure refrain?
The children's laughter, a curious sound,
In a world where his heart was bound.
A child's voice, sweet and bright,
Calls to him, breaking through the night.
"Come play with us," the invitation clear,
A simple gesture that draws him near.
He hesitates, then takes a step,
Toward the joy he's long kept.
The park transforms with each stride,
From a place of shadows to one of pride.
The colors bloom, the air feels light,
As he ventures further into the sight.
The laughter grows, a rising tide,
Pulling him from his past's dark side.
He joins their game, unsure and shy,
His laughter mingles with the sky.
The children's joy, a balm so pure,

Turns his pain into something sure.
Each shout, each cheer, a melody,
That unlocks his heart's deep plea.
The games are simple, the rules are clear,
Yet they weave a tapestry dear.
Tag and chase, and hide-and-seek,
The moments fleeting, but unique.
He finds himself in their embrace,
A refuge in their playful space.
In the circle of their innocent glee,
He feels a part of something free.
The weight of his grief begins to fade,
In the warmth of the games they've made.
The park, once a somber place,
Is now a haven of light and grace.
The past's dark grip starts to wane,
As he loses himself in the refrain.
His steps grow lighter, his heart beats fast,
In the joy of the present, his sorrows pass.
The children's laughter becomes his guide,
A path to healing, open wide.
The warmth of their laughter, a new dawn's light,
Breaks the hold of the endless night.
He feels a shift, a gentle sway,
As hope begins to light his way.
Their voices, like a soothing stream,
Wash away the remnants of his dream.

He reaches out to touch the breeze,
The rustling leaves, a quiet tease.
The world around him starts to sing,
A symphony of hope, a new beginning.
The park's transformation, a vivid hue,
Reflects the change he's passing through.
He watches as the sun dips low,
The park now bathed in evening's glow.
The children's joy, a constant sound,
Turns his fears into the ground.
The laughter, once a distant call,
Is now a melody that heals his fall.
As dusk approaches, he takes a breath,
Feeling the shift from sorrow to heft.
The joy he's found is not just fleeting,
But a beacon for his heart's new beating.
He's found a place where he can mend,
A future bright, a path to ascend.
In the park, where children play,
He's found a spark to light his way.
The echoes of their laughter bright,
Guide him through the coming night.
The park, once dark, now shines so clear,
As the children's joy draws him near.
With each day, he learns anew,
The strength to face what's tried and true.
In their laughter, he sees the dawn,

A future where his fears are gone.
The children's joy, a guiding star,
Leads him to the light, no matter how far.
In the quiet of the evening's grace,
He reflects on the joyful space.
The park has become his healing ground,
Where lost hope and peace are found.
In the children's laughter, he's set free,
A new chapter begins, full of possibility.
In the twilight of the park's embrace,
He takes a moment to find his place.
The laughter lingers, soft and bright,
As stars begin to pierce the night.
He reflects on the day's sweet grace,
The healing found in their playful space.
The air is cool, the sky aglow,
With hues of dusk, a gentle show.
The children's voices now a memory,
A light that guides him to serenity.
He watches as they bid farewell,
Their joy a story he'll retell.
The park's tranquility wraps around,
A sanctuary where peace is found.
The shadows lengthen, the day turns dark,
But within, a new hope leaves its mark.
He feels a shift, a newfound peace,
A promise that his fears will cease.

He walks alone beneath the stars,
A heart transformed, healing scars.
The park, once a place of gloom,
Is now a garden of renewed bloom.
He carries their laughter in his heart,
A melody to help him restart.
The children's joy, a vibrant thread,
Weaves through his thoughts, a path ahead.
He feels the warmth of the day's embrace,
A gentle touch in the moon's soft grace.
Each step he takes is light and free,
Guided by the park's sweet symphony.
In the quiet night, he makes a vow,
To cherish the joy he's found somehow.
To carry the laughter, pure and bright,
Into his days and darkest night.
The echoes of the children's cheer,
Are a beacon that draws him near.
The park, with its laughter, becomes a part
Of his journey, a balm for his heart.
In the moments of silence, he'll find
The strength to leave the past behind.
The children's voices, a distant song,
Will guide him as he moves along.
As the stars rise in the sky so high,
He feels a new hope gently nigh.
The park's embrace, both gentle and kind,

Is a reminder of the light he'll find.
He walks away with a heart renewed,
A spirit once again imbued.
The laughter of children, soft and clear,
Will remain with him, always near.
In their joy, he's found a way,
To brighten the darkest of his days.
The park, a place of healing and light,
Has given him strength to face the night.
In the chapters that follow, he'll carry this light,
Guided by the laughter that shines so bright.
The children's joy, a steadfast guide,
Will lead him through the shifting tide.
With every step, he'll move towards the dawn,
Embracing the new path he's drawn.
The park, a symbol of joy restored,
Will echo in his heart, forever adored.
In the laughter and light, he finds his peace,
A promise that his suffering will cease.
Chapter by chapter, he'll continue to mend,
With the children's laughter as his friend.
And so, he leaves the park behind,
With a hopeful heart and a peaceful mind.
The children's laughter, a cherished song,
Will guide him as he moves along.
In the quiet of the night's embrace,
He carries forward with renewed grace.

As he ventures forth from the park's embrace,
The stars above cast a soft trace.
He feels the night's gentle, cool caress,
A reminder of the day's bright success.
The echoes of laughter gently fade,
Yet their warmth in his heart is stayed.
The journey ahead seems less forlorn,
His spirit, once shattered, is reborn.
The path that once seemed dark and steep
Now glows with hope, where shadows creep.
The laughter he heard, a guiding star,
Illuminates the way, no matter how far.
With each step, he senses a change,
The world around him feels less strange.
The children's voices, a distant sound,
Are a melody that lifts him off the ground.
Their joy, a spark that lights his way,
Turns the night into a brighter day.
He pauses to reflect on the moments passed,
The feelings of joy that he's amassed.
The park, with its vibrant play and cheer,
Has left a mark that will persevere.
He carries their laughter, like a gentle breeze,
A reminder of peace and newfound ease.
As the night deepens and shadows stretch,
He feels a connection, a silent fetch.
The park's transformation in his soul,

Is a reminder that he can be whole.
The laughter, a gift he'll always keep,
A beacon to guide him through the deep.
The path ahead is filled with light,
A contrast to the previous night.
He moves with purpose, step by step,
Guided by the joy he's adept.
The children's laughter, a timeless thread,
Weaves through his thoughts, where hope is spread.
In the quiet moments of solitude,
He finds strength in the laughter's mood.
The memories of the park's bright hue,
Fill him with courage, strong and true.
He feels the past's grip start to slack,
As he moves forward, never looking back.
The journey ahead is unknown and vast,
But he walks with a heart steadfast.
The park's joy and laughter, a guiding light,
Will lead him through the darkest night.
Each step he takes is filled with grace,
As he embraces the future's face.
In dreams, he'll revisit the park's serene,
A place where hope and joy convene.
The children's laughter will forever ring,
A melody of hope, a hopeful spring.
Their voices will guide him through the night,
Towards a future that feels just right.

As dawn approaches, the stars grow faint,
The park's embrace has left its saint.
He walks with a heart both light and free,
A spirit renewed, a soul to be.
The children's laughter, pure and bright,
Is his beacon through the coming light.
In the quiet of the morning's grace,
He carries forward, a gentle pace.
The park's memory, a treasured song,
Will guide him as he moves along.
With each new day, he'll find his way,
Embracing the light, come what may.
The journey continues, filled with hope,
With the children's laughter to help him cope.
The park's transformation, a chapter complete,
Is a testament to the joy he'll meet.
With every step, he'll carry the cheer,
The laughter that brought him here.
In the tapestry of life's new dawn,
He'll weave the joy that he's drawn.
The children's laughter, a gift so rare,
Will guide him through with tender care.
And as he steps into the day's embrace,
He carries forward with a heart of grace.
As morning unfurls its golden light,
He steps forward, renewed by the night.
The park's echoes linger, soft and clear,

A melody that draws ever near.
The laughter of children, now a guide,
Shines a path through the day's rising tide.
In the heart of the city, where life moves fast,
He finds moments to pause and grasp.
The joy from the park, a gentle force,
Carries him along his new course.
Each interaction, a chance to spread
The warmth he found, the path he's led.
The bustling streets, once overwhelming,
Now seem less daunting, less unsettling.
The laughter's echo, a calming wave,
Transforms the chaos into a peaceful haven.
He greets each day with a lighter soul,
A heart now whole, a spirit whole.
At work, among the crowded throng,
He shares his joy through words and song.
The park's transformation is his own,
A story of healing, gently shown.
His colleagues notice, their eyes perceive,
The shift within, the way he weaves.
He engages more, his laughter genuine,
A reflection of the joy that's risen.
The children's laughter, a precious seed,
Grows within him, fulfilling a need.
The simple acts of kindness and care,
Reflect the love that he now dares.

On weekends, he returns to the park,
Where memories of laughter leave their mark.
He watches the children, now a friend,
Their joy a message that will never end.
He joins their games, their laughter soars,
Healing the remnants of past wars.
He feels the change with each passing day,
The past's shadows slowly decay.
The children's laughter, a cherished tune,
Guides him through the afternoon.
In their playful world, he finds his place,
A sanctuary of joy and grace.
As seasons shift and years unfold,
He carries the laughter, a story told.
The park's magic, a constant guide,
Through life's journey, far and wide.
The children's voices, pure and bright,
Remain a beacon in the night.
He finds peace in the simple things,
In the joy that each new day brings.
The laughter he once sought to escape,
Now frames his world, a joyous shape.
In every smile, in every cheer,
He hears the echoes of what's dear.
In moments of solitude and rest,
He reflects on the day's true test.
The park's gift, a reminder of light,

Guides him through each darkened night.
He carries the laughter, a precious guide,
A source of strength that will not hide.
As the days blend into years,
He looks back with grateful tears.
The park's laughter, a constant thread,
Weaves through the life he's led.
Each chapter written, each step embraced,
Is touched by the joy that's been traced.
He lives his life with newfound zeal,
Embracing the joy that he can feel.
The children's laughter, a song of grace,
Guides him through life's vast space.
In their cheer, he finds his way,
To a brighter, more hopeful day.
The park's transformation, a story complete,
Is a testament to the joy he'll meet.
With every step, he'll carry the light,
The laughter that turned his darkest night.
In every sunrise, in every dawn,
He carries the laughter, a joy reborn.
In the tapestry of time and space,
The park's laughter leaves its trace.
A gift of joy, a cherished friend,
Guides him through life until the end.
And as he walks into the future bright,
He carries the laughter, a guiding light.

The park, a sacred realm of light,
Becomes a symbol of his inner fight.
He visits often, where memories weave,
A comfort in the life he now believes.
The echoes of laughter, vivid and clear,
Guide him through moments of doubt and fear.
In the changing seasons, as leaves fall and rise,
He sees the park's reflection in the skies.
The cycles of nature mirror his own,
A journey from darkness to light fully grown.
Each season's turn, a metaphor shared,
For the healing process, tenderly prepared.
The winter's chill, the spring's first bloom,
The summer's warmth, the autumn's gloom,
Each season brings its own array,
Of challenges and joy along the way.
The children's laughter, a constant sound,
Weaves through the seasons, profound.
In winter's frost, he finds a peace,
A quiet place where worries cease.
The laughter of children, though distant now,
Still warms his heart, a gentle vow.
The snowflakes fall, soft and light,
Reflecting the joy of past delight.
As spring arrives, with buds and blooms,
He feels the park's renewing tunes.
The laughter grows, fresh and bright,

In the rebirth of the season's light.
He embraces the world with open arms,
Welcomed by spring's gentle charms.
Summer brings a vibrant flare,
With long, bright days and warmer air.
He returns to the park, where children play,
Their laughter a soundtrack to each day.
The warmth of summer, a joyful friend,
Embraces him as seasons blend.
In autumn's embrace, with leaves of gold,
He reflects on the story told.
The children's laughter, now a cherished song,
Guides him as he moves along.
The park, a canvas of shifting hues,
Echoes the joy and the peace he pursues.
As years go by, the park remains,
A timeless place where joy sustains.
The laughter of children, a constant guide,
Helps him navigate life's changing tide.
Each visit to the park, a return to grace,
A reminder of his healing space.
In the twilight of his journey's end,
The park's laughter remains a friend.
He looks back with a heart full of peace,
Grateful for the joy that will never cease.
The children's laughter, forever near,
Is a melody he'll always hold dear.

He leaves the park with a heart fulfilled,
The echoes of laughter, forever instilled.
The journey from darkness to light,
Is marked by the joy of children's delight.
In every step, in every breath,
He carries the laughter beyond death.
The park's gift, a symbol of cheer,
Guides him through each passing year.
The laughter of children, a beacon bright,
Leads him through the darkest night.
In every sunrise, in every dawn,
He carries the joy that he's drawn.
The park, a testament to his past,
Will forever in his heart last.
The children's laughter, pure and true,
Is a reminder of the light he knew.
And as he journeys through the days ahead,
He'll carry the laughter where it's led.
In the quiet moments, he'll hear the sound,
Of laughter's echoes all around.
The park's joy, a constant friend,
Will guide him as he transcends.
And in the story of his life's embrace,
The laughter of children will find its place.
As he continues through the tapestry of life,
The park's memories become his guiding light.
The laughter of children, a soothing refrain,

Echoes through his days, easing the strain.
Each playful moment, each joyful sound,
Transcends the shadows that once were profound.
He finds himself drawn to the park's embrace,
A refuge where he can find his place.
The children's games, their boundless cheer,
Create a sanctuary, a world sincere.
The park, a canvas of joy and mirth,
Reveals the beauty in life's rebirth.
With each season's turn, he learns to grow,
Embracing the changes, letting go.
The children's laughter, a constant thread,
Weaves through the fabric of the life he's led.
Their innocence and delight, a source of peace,
Offer solace, and his worries cease.
As he walks through the park, he sees anew,
The world through a lens of vibrant hue.
The laughter of children becomes his guide,
Leading him to a place where hope resides.
Their joy, a beacon in the vast expanse,
Encourages him to take a chance.
In moments of solitude and reflection,
He draws strength from the park's connection.
The echoes of laughter, a gentle call,
Remind him that he can stand tall.
The park's enchantment, a reminder true,
That joy and healing can always renew.

He cherishes the park as a sacred ground,
A place where lost souls can be found.
The children's laughter, a timeless song,
Echoes the truth that he now belongs.
In their games and cheer, he finds his way,
A path to light, through night and day.
In the quiet evenings, when shadows play,
He reflects on the journey, on the fray.
The park's memories, vivid and bright,
Illuminate his path through the night.
The laughter of children, a guiding star,
Leads him to places both near and far.
He shares his story with those he meets,
Spreading the joy that the park completes.
The laughter of children, a tale so sweet,
Inspires others to rise to their feet.
He becomes a beacon of hope and grace,
Reflecting the joy he found in this place.
In the twilight of his journey's close,
He carries the laughter, as the river flows.
The park's gift, a melody of cheer,
Guides him through the final frontier.
The children's laughter, a constant guide,
Leads him to where his dreams reside.
As he leaves the park, a heart at peace,
He knows the laughter will never cease.
The joy of children, a gift so rare,

Will remain with him, beyond compare.
In every smile, in every cheer,
He'll find the echoes of what is dear.
In the realm of dreams and morning's light,
The park's laughter will forever ignite.
A source of comfort, a guiding hand,
In the journey through life's shifting sand.
The children's laughter, a melody bright,
Will guide him through the darkest night.
And as he walks into the days ahead,
With the laughter of children gently spread,
He knows that in every moment, near and far,
The park's joy will be his guiding star.
In the dance of life, in the whispering breeze,
He'll carry the laughter, and find his ease.
The park's enchantment, a story so profound,
Will remain in his heart, forever bound.
The children's laughter, a timeless embrace,
Guides him through life with grace.
And as he journeys on, through twilight and dawn,
The laughter of the park will lead him on.
As he ventures deeper into the fabric of life,
The park remains his beacon through both joy and strife.
The laughter of children, a harmonious tune,
Guides him through nights and the glow of noon.
In their joy, he finds his own,
A reminder of the seeds he's sown.

He walks through the park with an open heart,
Embracing the beauty, a brand new start.
The children's laughter, a vibrant chord,
Plays a melody that he cannot ignore.
It fills the air with a sense of peace,
A balm that helps his worries cease.
In the midst of their games, he discovers more,
A reflection of himself from days of yore.
The innocence and wonder in their eyes,
Unveil the strength he thought had died.
He sees his own past in their playful spree,
A connection that sets his spirit free.
He watches as they run and leap,
Their carefree spirits a promise to keep.
The park, a place of endless cheer,
Becomes a canvas where his fears disappear.
Each laughter-filled moment a piece of grace,
In the tapestry of his healing space.
The children's world, so full and bright,
Teaches him to embrace the light.
Their joy, untainted by the past,
Shows him that happiness can last.
He learns from their boundless delight,
That the darkest days can still turn bright.
In the afternoons, beneath the trees,
He finds solace in the gentle breeze.
The park's tranquility, a soothing balm,

Turns his once tempestuous world calm.
He sits and listens to the laughter's song,
Feeling a sense of where he belongs.
As twilight descends, the laughter fades,
Yet the park's magic never degrades.
He leaves with a heart rejuvenated,
His soul once weary, now elated.
The children's laughter, a guiding flame,
Keeps him hopeful, free from shame.
He reflects on the journey, the path he's trod,
And finds gratitude in the park's façade.
The laughter of children, pure and clear,
Is a gift he holds forever near.
It becomes a symbol of strength and grace,
Guiding him through every space.
In the quiet of the evening, as stars ignite,
He feels the warmth of the children's light.
Their laughter lingers in the twilight air,
A reminder that joy is always there.
He carries their echoes as he moves ahead,
Finding comfort in the laughter he's been fed.
The park's laughter becomes a sacred hymn,
A melody of hope that never grows dim.
As he journeys on, through every trial,
He finds strength in their innocent smile.
The children's joy, a timeless embrace,
Guides him through each new place.

He finds renewal in the echoes of cheer,
A source of comfort that's always near.
The park, with its laughter and play,
Becomes a beacon that lights his way.
In every laugh, in every cheer,
He finds the strength to persevere.
And so he walks, with heart renewed,
Guided by the laughter he's pursued.
The park's gift, a joy so deep,
Is a promise that he'll always keep.
In every moment, in every smile,
He carries the laughter, mile after mile.
The children's laughter, a song so sweet,
Will always be a guide, a beacon, a treat.
In the tapestry of his life's embrace,
Their joy will forever hold its place.
As he moves forward, through each new day,
The laughter of the park will light his way.
The park becomes a world apart,
A sanctuary for his mending heart.
With each visit, the shadows recede,
Replaced by the laughter that he so needs.
The children's voices, a symphony of grace,
Carry him to a cherished place.
In the quiet moments, as dusk descends,
He feels the magic that never ends.
The park, bathed in the glow of twilight's hue,

Transforms into a realm both fresh and new.
The laughter of children, a soft refrain,
Whispers of joy, releasing his pain.
He sees the park as a mirror to his soul,
Reflecting the healing that makes him whole.
The joy of the children, unfiltered and bright,
Becomes a beacon in the dark of night.
Their carefree spirits, a living song,
Guide him where his heart belongs.
He learns to dance with their playful glee,
Finding solace in their boundless spree.
Each leap, each bound, a step toward the light,
A reminder that even shadows can be bright.
The park's enchantment, a precious gift,
Lifts him from his sorrow's drift.
As the seasons change, the park evolves,
But its essence remains, the joy it resolves.
He witnesses the cycles of nature's hand,
And feels a connection to the land.
The children's laughter, ever near,
Guides him through each shifting year.
In the winter's chill and summer's blaze,
The park's spirit continues to amaze.
The laughter of children, a constant cheer,
Warms his heart through each passing year.
The park becomes a timeless realm,
Where hope and joy are at the helm.

He takes comfort in the park's embrace,
A refuge where he finds his place.
The laughter of children, a song so pure,
Offers a healing that's sure.
He carries their joy through life's vast sea,
Finding peace in their melody.
The park's essence seeps into his soul,
Making him feel once again whole.
He shares the laughter with those he meets,
Spreading joy through the city streets.
The children's happiness becomes his own,
A gift that's cherished, a treasure known.
In the still of the night, beneath the stars,
He reflects on the journey that has brought him far.
The park's laughter, a guiding light,
Illuminates his path through the night.
He feels the echoes of their joy within,
A reminder of the peace he's found again.
The park's gift is a constant refrain,
A source of comfort through the strain.
As he moves forward, through joy and sorrow,
He knows the laughter will guide him tomorrow.
The children's voices, a beacon bright,
Lead him through the darkest night.
In every step, in every breath,
He finds the laughter that outshines death.
The park, a haven of joy so true,

Becomes a part of all he'll do.
The children's laughter, a melody sweet,
Is a companion on his journey's beat.
He leaves the park with a heart uplifted,
Grateful for the joy that's been gifted.
The laughter of children, a timeless embrace,
Guides him through life with grace.
And as he steps into the future's light,
The park's joy will forever shine bright.
In every moment, in every cheer,
The echoes of laughter will always be near.
The children's joy, a guiding star,
Will lead him through life, no matter how far.
The park's laughter, a song so deep,
Will be his companion in every leap.
As he continues to walk through life's expanse,
The park's echoes guide him in every chance.
The laughter of children, a constant reminder,
That even in darkness, light grows finer.
Their joy, a force that transcends time,
Imparts a rhythm, a healing rhyme.
The seasons shift, but the park remains,
A timeless realm where joy sustains.
Each cycle of the year brings new delight,
Yet the laughter persists, a guiding light.
The children's voices weave through the air,
A symphony of hope, a balm for despair.

Spring's renewal, with its vibrant blooms,
Mirrors the laughter that chases gloom.
Summer's warmth, with its golden rays,
Echoes the joy of their carefree plays.
Autumn's crisp air, with its rustling leaves,
Reflects the laughter that never grieves.
Winter's chill, with its silent grace,
Holds the laughter in a gentle embrace.
The snowflakes fall with a soft, serene sound,
A reminder of the joy that's always around.
In every season, the park remains,
A sanctuary where happiness sustains.
He finds solace in the park's eternal charm,
A refuge from life's tumultuous storm.
The children's laughter, a melody sweet,
Carries him through life's challenging feat.
Their joy, a beacon that lights his way,
Guides him through each coming day.
The park becomes a canvas for his soul,
A place where fragments of joy make him whole.
He finds renewal in its endless embrace,
A sanctuary where he can find his place.
The children's laughter, a timeless thread,
Woven into the tapestry of life ahead.
In every corner of the park, he sees,
The echoes of laughter in the rustling trees.
The swings sway gently, the slides shine bright,

Reflecting the joy that dispels the night.
The park's essence, a constant guide,
Leads him through life's shifting tide.
He shares the laughter with those around,
Spreading joy wherever he is found.
The park's magic becomes a part of him,
A light that never grows dim.
The children's joy, a gift so rare,
Fills his heart with tender care.
In the quiet moments, he reflects on the grace,
The park has brought to his space.
The laughter of children, a guiding star,
Lights his path, no matter how far.
He finds peace in their carefree play,
A reminder that joy is never far away.
As he moves forward, the park remains,
A constant source of joy through gains and pains.
The children's laughter, a song so dear,
Guides him through each passing year.
In every smile, in every cheer,
He finds the strength to persevere.
The park's laughter is a treasure profound,
A melody that forever surrounds.
In every season, in every hour,
He finds the joy that holds power.
The children's laughter, a timeless embrace,
Guides him through life's intricate space.

In the end, he carries the park's cheer,
A beacon of light that's always near.
The laughter of children, pure and bright,
Shines through the darkest night.
The park's joy becomes his guide,
A companion through life's every stride.
And as he looks to the future's gleam,
The laughter remains a cherished dream.
The park, with its laughter and play,
Becomes a part of his every day.
In the echoes of joy, he finds his way,
Guided by laughter, come what may.
As the years roll on, the park stands still,
A beacon of joy, a place of will.
The laughter of children, a timeless sound,
Spreads its warmth all around.
The seasons turn, the years advance,
Yet the park remains, a place of chance.
He returns often, to the park's embrace,
To find solace in its gentle space.
The laughter of children, like a soothing balm,
Brings a sense of peace, a calming calm.
Their joy, a thread that weaves through his days,
Guides him through life's shifting maze.
In the springtime's bloom, he feels reborn,
As the park awakens with the dawn.
The children's laughter, a call to play,

Brings a light to his every day.
He joins their games, with renewed zest,
Finding a joy that feels like a quest.
Summer's warmth brings a golden glow,
A time when the laughter continues to flow.
The park is alive with vibrant hues,
Reflecting the joy he continues to choose.
He feels the sun's embrace, so warm,
As the children's laughter becomes the norm.
Autumn arrives with its tapestry bright,
A canvas of colors in the fading light.
The park is adorned in hues of gold,
A testament to the joy he holds.
The laughter of children mingles with the breeze,
A symphony of joy that puts him at ease.
Winter's chill, with its quiet grace,
Brings a serene calm to the park's face.
The snow-covered ground, a pristine sheet,
Reflects the laughter that's warm and sweet.
He walks through the snow, feeling at peace,
As the park's joy provides a gentle release.
Throughout the seasons, the park remains,
A constant source of joy amidst life's strains.
The children's laughter, a guiding force,
Helps him navigate life's uncertain course.
In their presence, he finds a spark,
A reminder that joy can light up the dark.

He learns to appreciate the simple things,
The laughter of children, the joy it brings.
The park becomes a sanctuary, a place of grace,
Where he finds solace in its warm embrace.
The children's joy, a gift so grand,
Becomes a beacon he can always stand.
In quiet moments, he reflects with pride,
On the journey the laughter has guided.
The park's gift, a constant refrain,
Brings him comfort through joy and pain.
The children's laughter, a melody pure,
Is a promise that his heart can endure.
As he grows older, the park stays true,
A place where his dreams come into view.
The laughter of children continues to play,
Guiding him through each passing day.
In the echoes of joy, he finds his way,
A reminder of light amidst the gray.
The park's essence remains a cherished part,
A sanctuary for his heart.
The children's laughter, a timeless song,
Guides him through life, where he belongs.
He carries their joy wherever he roams,
Finding peace in the laughter that he calls home.
In the final days, he looks back and sees,
The park's laughter as a gentle breeze.
The joy of children, a guiding light,

That led him through the darkest night.
The park, with its endless cheer,
Becomes a part of him, always near.
As he rests beneath the park's wide sky,
He feels the laughter, as time goes by.
The children's joy, a song of grace,
Guides him to his final resting place.
The park remains a beacon bright,
A testament to joy's enduring light.
In every breeze, in every sound,
He feels the laughter all around.
The park's gift, a constant friend,
Guides him through life's final end.
The children's laughter, pure and clear,
Is a melody he holds dear.
As he lies beneath the park's wide sky,
The echoes of laughter drift on by.
He closes his eyes and feels the air,
A gentle breeze that shows it cares.
In the laughter of children, pure and free,
He finds a sense of eternity.
For though his days are drawing near,
Their joy remains, a voice so clear.
The world around him moves with grace,
As if the park itself is a sacred space.
He recalls the way the children played,
How their laughter never seemed to fade.

Each shout, each cheer, a symphony,
A timeless song that let him be.
He breathes in deeply, and with that breath,
He feels the park has conquered death.
The sun begins its slow descent,
Casting shadows where light once went.
Yet even as the day turns to night,
The park remains bathed in soft, warm light.
The laughter lingers in the air,
A gentle hum beyond compare.
It fills his soul, it fills his mind,
A comfort that is sweet and kind.
In his quiet moments, he starts to dream,
Of life beyond, a brighter gleam.
The park, the children, the joy they bring,
Become the echoes of everything.
For though his time may soon be past,
The children's joy will ever last.
Their laughter, a melody so sweet,
Becomes the rhythm of his heart's beat.
And even when the night grows cold,
The laughter keeps his spirit bold.
In the starlight's quiet, soft embrace,
He finds a warmth in this sacred place.
The children's laughter, once distant and low,
Now fills him with a steady glow.
Each sound a promise, a whispered vow,

That life and joy are here and now.
The trees around him sway with ease,
Their branches dancing in the breeze.
The leaves, like children, rustle and sing,
A chorus of life in everything.
He listens closely, feels the beat,
Of life's grand dance beneath his feet.
The children's laughter, a guiding sound,
Keeps his spirit heaven-bound.
In every rustle of the trees,
In every sigh within the breeze,
He hears the children's voices soar,
Reminding him there's always more.
The park, alive with sounds and sights,
Becomes a beacon of soft delights.
And even as his breath grows slow,
The park's embrace won't let him go.
The moon now rises in the sky,
Casting silver light where shadows lie.
Yet in the moon's soft, glowing hue,
The children's laughter remains true.
It weaves itself into the night,
A sound so pure, so full of light.
He feels it cradle him, so near,
A melody he holds so dear.
The park, once a place of solace found,
Now becomes sacred ground.

For in its bounds, he learned to see,
The truth in joy, the way to be.
The children's laughter, once a sound,
Now echoes through him, all around.
It fills the air, it fills the sky,
A song that never says goodbye.
And as the night begins to fall,
He hears the final, gentle call.
The children's laughter, soft and light,
Guides him through the darkest night.
It leads him to a place of peace,
Where all his worries, all fears cease.
He closes his eyes with a gentle sigh,
And lets the laughter carry him high.
The park remains, its heart aglow,
A place where endless joy will flow.
The children's laughter, forever bright,
Guides the world into the light.
Though he may rest beneath the trees,
His spirit dances in the breeze.
For in their laughter, he found his way,
To endless night and endless day.

A Final Glimpse of Joy

As the stars take their place in the dark, wide sky,
The park below is lit by fireflies.
Their soft glow dances through the air,
A shimmering light, a promise so rare.

The children's laughter blends with the night,
Their joy, a beacon, forever bright.
The fireflies' glow, the stars' calm grace,
Create a timeless, sacred space.
The laughter of children, forever it rings,
A reminder of all the little things.
In the simple joy of their carefree play,
He found the strength to face the day.
The world moves on, the seasons turn,
But the park's gentle spirit will always burn.
And in the laughter of those who run,
The essence of life, a race well won.
Even as time stretches on and on,
The laughter of children greets each dawn.
The park remains a sacred site,
Where joy and peace forever unite.
And though the years may come and go,
The children's laughter continues to grow.
A symbol of hope, a song of grace,
That leaves its mark on every place.
The park, once dark, now shines so bright,
A testament to life's pure light.
For in the laughter of youth so pure,
He found the strength to endure.
And though his journey may now be done,
The children's joy lives on like the sun.
A reminder that no matter how deep,

There's always laughter to keep.

<u>The Circle of Laughter</u>

Generations pass, and still they come,
To the park where laughter hums.
Children chase and children play,
Filling the park with light each day.
Their laughter echoes, soft and clear,
A sound that drives away all fear.
And though he's gone, his spirit remains,
In every laugh, in every refrain.
The children run with boundless grace,
Carrying joy to every place.
And in the trees, the wind sings too,
A song of life, of something true.
The park becomes a sacred thread,
Weaving the living with the dead.
And through it all, the laughter flows,
A river of joy that never slows.
In this place, where laughter reigns,
He found the way to break his chains.
The park, with its trees and open sky,
Became the place where he learned to fly.
For in the children's laughter pure,
He found the strength to endure.
And though his journey is now complete,
The laughter remains, forever sweet.
The park, once a refuge from despair,

Becomes a home for all who care.
The children's laughter, a sacred sound,
Reminds the world of joy unbound.
And as the days and nights go by,
Their joy will never die.
With the final echoes of the children's play,
The park becomes his eternal stay.
And in the wind, so soft and kind,
The whispers of laughter forever bind.

7. A Glimmer of Hope

As days pass by, he starts to see,
The world anew, with clarity.
The burdens he once thought his own,
Begin to lift, as seeds are sown.
Each smile, each laugh, a step ahead,
Away from the past, from all he dreads.
The park becomes his sacred place,
A refuge from his darkened space.
Yet, the glimmer of hope isn't always steady.
There are mornings when the weight still lingers,
When the old ghosts of memory return, uninvited.
The park, though now a sanctuary,
Holds echoes of the days before the pain,
Reminders of a time when the shadows
Were only things that passed with the dusk.
Now, as he walks these familiar paths,
He realizes that healing isn't linear—
It ebbs and flows, rises and falls,
Like the tides that tug at his inner shore.
He feels the dawn, the rising sun,
A sign that life has just begun.
No longer trapped by night's embrace,

He finds his stride, his steady pace.
But even in this newfound light,
The dark edges of the past remain in sight.
They don't vanish, but they fade,
Like the thinning mist at the break of day.
Some Days are Still Heavy
There are days when the weight of yesterday
Rests heavily on his chest.
Days when the laughter of children in the park
Isn't enough to silence the echo of his loss.
But those days are fewer now,
And when they come,
He knows they will pass.
For in his heart, a new resilience grows,
Fed by the warmth of each morning's light.
He understands now that the path forward
Isn't about escaping the shadows entirely,
But about learning to live alongside them,
To let the light filter through the cracks,
And to trust that the moments of joy
Will outlast the moments of sorrow.
Hope, a glimmer, now shines bright,
Guiding him through the darkest night.
In each new day, a promise made,
That shadows, in time, will surely fade.
Small Acts of Renewal
He begins to notice the little things—

The way the leaves shimmer in the morning light,
The soft rustling of the breeze through the trees,
The sound of his own footsteps on the earth,
Each one a reminder that he's still here,
Still moving forward, still alive.
He starts to engage with the world again—
Not just as a spectator, but as a participant.
He joins in conversations, even if just briefly.
He allows himself to smile without guilt,
To laugh without the weight of sorrow.
Each of these moments, though small,
Feel like victories.
The world, once dim, now bursts with light,
A new beginning, a future bright.
The People Around Him
At first, he hadn't noticed them—
The people who passed by,
The ones who lingered in the park.
But now, he starts to see their faces,
To recognize their presence.
There's the elderly man who sits on the same bench,
The woman who jogs every morning with her dog,
The mother who watches her children play.
They are all part of this new world
He is slowly coming to embrace.
He doesn't speak to them,
But their presence grounds him.

It reminds him that life goes on,
And that he, too, can be part of it.
The weight of sorrow, once so deep,
Begins to lift, the wounds start to sleep.
In every dawn, in every ray,
He finds the strength to face the day.

The Power of Routine

He establishes a routine—
Walking through the park in the early mornings,
Sitting beneath the same tree as the sun rises.
There's a comfort in the rhythm of it,
In the predictability of these quiet moments.
Each day feels like a small step forward,
Away from the shadows of the past.
The park's embrace, so warm, so kind,
Offers solace to his troubled mind.
In its beauty, he starts to heal,
His heart begins to gently feel.

The Shift Inside Him

One day, as he sits on his usual bench,
Watching the world move around him,
He realizes something has shifted within him.
It's not a grand revelation,
But a quiet, subtle change—
A softening of the hard edges of his grief,
A loosening of the tight grip
That sorrow once held on his heart.

He no longer feels like he's drowning.
The dark waters of despair
Have receded, leaving room for something new.
It's not a complete transformation,
But it's enough—enough to feel lighter,
Enough to feel like he's finally
Moving toward a future
Where the pain doesn't define him.
Each step he takes is filled with grace,
As he moves away from his darkened space.
The glimmer of hope, a guiding star,
Leads him forward, no longer marred.

Looking Forward

He begins to make plans—
Not grand plans, but simple ones.
Maybe he'll take up a hobby,
Visit the cafe he used to love,
Rekindle old friendships.
These thoughts don't overwhelm him now,
As they once did.
Instead, they feel like possibilities,
Like doors opening
To a world he thought he had lost.
He celebrates the victories small,
In every moment, he stands tall.
Hope is a beacon, shining clear,
Leading him to a life sincere.

The path ahead, though still unknown,
Is now a journey he's not alone.
With hope as his guide, he'll forge his way,
Towards a brighter, hopeful day.
The days move forward, each one brighter than the last,
Though the path has been winding, with moments that feel slow,
The glimmer of hope has turned into something more solid,
A small flame that now refuses to be extinguished.
The man who once felt swallowed by shadows
Now begins to see light in places he never expected.

A New Perspective

He walks through the same park,
But something in his perception has changed.
Where he once saw only the grayness of the trees,
He now notices the vibrant hues of green
As the leaves catch the morning sun.
The flowers in bloom seem more vivid,
And the sounds of the birds overhead
No longer irritate him,
But instead bring a strange sense of peace.
He realizes that these sights and sounds
Have always been there—
He just couldn't see them before.
Grief had clouded his vision,
Sorrow had dulled his senses.
But now, as if a fog has lifted,
The world feels sharper,

More alive, more welcoming.
It's not that the pain is gone—
It still lingers in the corners of his heart—
But it no longer controls him.
The Healing Power of Connection
As he walks, he starts to recognize familiar faces—
The same people who come to the park day after day.
The jogger with her dog, the elderly man reading a book,
The mother and her children who laugh and play.
He feels an unexpected connection to them,
Though he has never spoken a word.
One day, as he sits on a bench,
The elderly man looks up from his book
And gives him a small nod.
It's a simple gesture,
But it fills him with warmth.
There's an unspoken understanding between them,
As if the man knows, in some way,
That he too is healing.
The nod is a sign of solidarity,
Of shared experience,
A reminder that even in solitude,
He is not truly alone.
*****The Meaning in Small Moments*****
Each day, the man looks forward to his morning walks,
His time in the park has become a ritual,
A grounding moment in his day.

He begins to notice more details—
The way the sunlight filters through the trees,
The sound of children's laughter
That once felt so distant, so separate from his world,
Now feels like an invitation to live again.
He finds joy in the smallest things:
The feel of the breeze on his face,
The crunch of leaves beneath his shoes,
The soft chirping of birds high in the branches.
These moments, so ordinary,
Have become extraordinary to him.
The past still holds him at times,
But it no longer suffocates him.
He no longer feels trapped in the endless loop
Of sorrow and regret.
Instead, he allows himself to experience
The world around him,
To be present in a way he hasn't been for so long.
Revisiting the Past with New Eyes
One evening, as the sun sets and the sky
Turns shades of pink and gold,
He thinks back on his past,
On the years that had once felt lost.
For so long, he had only seen his life
Through the lens of what he had lost.
But now, something shifts within him.
He realizes that while the pain was real,

So too were the moments of joy,
The love, the laughter, the happiness
That had once filled his days.
The memories, though tinged with sorrow,
Now seem more balanced.
He can see both sides—
The light and the dark,
The joy and the pain—
And he no longer feels the need to deny
Either part of his story.
The Gentle Work of Healing
Healing, he understands now,
Isn't about erasing the past.
It's about integrating it,
Allowing it to coexist
With the present and the future.
The wounds don't disappear,
But they become softer,
Less raw, less consuming.
The scar is still there,
But it's no longer something
He feels he needs to hide.
The glimmer of hope that had started as a flicker
Has grown into something more substantial.
It's no longer fragile, no longer fleeting.
It's a steady presence within him,
A reminder that while the past will always be a part of him,

It doesn't define him.
He is more than his sorrow,
More than his grief.
He is someone who has lived through darkness,
And come out the other side.
The Future Begins to Take Shape
With this new understanding,
He starts to make plans.
Small, tentative plans,
But plans nonetheless.
Maybe he'll start visiting the café
He once loved,
Or take up painting,
A hobby he had abandoned long ago.
He's not in a rush,
But the fact that he's even considering
The possibility of the future
Feels like a victory.
He imagines what his life could look like,
Not in a grand, sweeping way,
But in the simple details of everyday existence—
The smell of coffee in the morning,
The warmth of the sun on his face,
The sound of his own laughter,
Genuine and unforced.
These are the things he wants to hold onto,
The things that feel like hope.

Hope is a beacon, shining clear,
Leading him to a life sincere.
The path ahead, though still unknown,
Is now a journey he's not alone.
With hope as his guide, he'll forge his way,
Towards a brighter, hopeful day.
The Park as a Sanctuary
He walks the familiar path through the park once more,
But now it feels different.
The park has become his sanctuary,
A place where time seems to slow down,
Where the world outside fades away,
Leaving only the sound of rustling leaves,
The gentle sway of the trees,
And the whispers of the wind that carry a sense of peace.
He begins to notice the regulars in the park—
The couple who walk hand in hand each evening,
The mother who pushes her stroller with quiet determination,
The children who seem to exist in a world
Untouched by sorrow or worry.
Their laughter fills the air,
And though it still tugs at his heart,
He no longer feels the sting of envy.
Instead, he finds a strange comfort in their presence,
As if their happiness is something
He can one day share in too.
The park, which once felt like an escape

From the overwhelming weight of his emotions,
Now feels like a place where those emotions
Can be gently cradled,
Not ignored, but held with care.
He realizes that healing doesn't mean
Forgetting or suppressing what he feels,
But rather learning to live with those feelings
In a way that doesn't consume him.
The Unfamiliar Feeling of Lightness
One morning, as he sits on his usual bench,
He feels something unfamiliar—
A lightness in his chest.
It's so subtle at first,
He wonders if he's imagining it.
But as the day goes on,
The feeling persists.
It's not joy, not quite,
But it's the absence of something darker.
It's the absence of the constant heaviness
That has weighed him down for so long.
He feels as though a small part of his soul
Has been freed,
A part he thought he had lost.
He tries not to question it too much,
Afraid that acknowledging it
Might make it disappear.
But as days pass,

The feeling grows stronger.
There are still moments of sadness,
Still nights when the shadows creep back in,
But they no longer define his existence.
There are now moments of reprieve,
Moments when he can breathe without the weight
Pressing down on him.
The Journey of Self-Compassion
He begins to understand the importance
Of being gentle with himself.
For so long, he had punished himself
For not being able to move on,
For not being able to let go of the past.
He had believed that healing
Should happen quickly,
That he should be able to rise above his pain
With strength and resilience.
But now, as he walks through the park,
He realizes that healing is not linear.
It is messy, unpredictable, and often slow.
There are good days and bad days,
Moments of progress and moments of setback.
And that's okay.
He starts to practice self-compassion,
To speak to himself in a way
That is kinder, more forgiving.
When the sadness comes,

He no longer berates himself
For feeling weak.
Instead, he allows the sadness to exist,
Acknowledges it,
And then gently lets it pass.
He learns to celebrate the small victories—
A day without tears,
A conversation with a stranger,
A moment of laughter.
These may seem insignificant,
But to him, they are monumental.
Hope Blossoming
As the days turn into weeks,
The glimmer of hope that had once been faint
Begins to blossom into something more.
It's still fragile,
Still something he holds carefully,
But it's there, growing stronger with each passing day.
He starts to think about the future,
About what his life could look like beyond the pain.
For the first time in what feels like forever,
He dares to dream.
The dreams are small at first—
A new hobby, a visit to a place he once loved,
A conversation with someone who might understand.
But these dreams, no matter how small,
Fill him with a sense of possibility

That had long been absent.
He begins to make plans,
Not just for surviving the days,
But for living them.
He thinks about the things that once brought him joy,
The people he used to love spending time with.
He's not quite ready to reach out,
Not quite ready to fully re-engage with the world,
But the thought no longer terrifies him.
Facing the Future
The future no longer feels like a dark,
Uncertain void.
It still holds its challenges,
Still feels daunting at times,
But it also holds promise.
There is room for growth,
For new experiences,
For new connections.
As he continues to walk through the park each day,
He starts to notice how the seasons are changing.
The air is crisper now,
The leaves have begun to fall,
Creating a golden carpet beneath his feet.
Change is happening all around him,
And for the first time in a long time,
He feels ready to change with it.
He doesn't know what the future holds,

But he no longer feels trapped by the past.
He can see a path ahead,
Not fully clear,
But visible enough to take the next step.
And that, he realizes,
Is enough.
A Moment of Realization
One day, as he stands by the edge of the park,
Watching the sun set in a blaze of orange and red,
He feels a sense of peace wash over him.
It's a fleeting moment,
But in that moment,
He knows that he is going to be okay.
The road ahead is still long,
And there will be more difficult days,
But he has found something within himself—
A strength, a resilience,
That he didn't know he had.
Hope is no longer just a glimmer.
It has become a steady light,
Guiding him through the darkness,
Lighting the way forward.
He smiles to himself,
A small, quiet smile,
And takes a deep breath.
He is ready for whatever comes next.

8. Lessons Learned

In the children's laughter, pure and true,
He finds the wisdom, old yet new.
Why dwell on loss, on what is past?
When life's true beauty is meant to last.
Amid the park's sprawling green,
Where sunlight dances, soft and serene,
He watches as the children play,
Their joy a beacon, guiding his way.
He feels the breeze, a gentle touch,
A whisper of peace, a soothing crutch.
Each gust a reminder, fleeting yet strong,
That time moves forward, life's sweet song.
He learns to let the sorrow go,
To find the peace in life's ebb and flow.
The tears once heavy now gently fade,
As he steps into the light, unafraid.
Each moment lived, a gift, a grace,
A chance to move from time's cold embrace.
He watches as the shadows lift,
Replaced by sunlight's warming gift.
The Weight of Expectation
The burden of expectation lifts slowly,

Like mist retreating with the morning sun.
He had always measured his worth
By the intensity of his pain,
Believing that healing should be swift,
That strength meant never faltering.
But as the days pass and the nights blend
Into a more gentle rhythm,
He recognizes that these measures
Are constructs of his own making,
Not the true path to peace.
The park becomes a metaphor,
Its seasons mirroring his inner change.
From the bare branches of winter's grief,
To the budding flowers of spring's renewal,
He understands now that healing
Is a season in itself,
With its own cycles of growth and rest.
Reconnecting with the World
In his newfound clarity, he begins
To reconnect with the world around him.
He takes tentative steps into old haunts,
A café he used to frequent, now warm and inviting,
Its aroma of coffee and pastries
A gentle reminder of simpler times.
He observes the barista, a young woman
With a perpetual smile, and finds
That even a brief exchange can spark

A sense of normalcy he had forgotten.
Small talk about the weather,
The latest news, the daily specials—
Each conversation, though fleeting,
Bridges the gap between isolation and community.
He revisits old hobbies, too,
Once abandoned, now rekindled with a soft eagerness.
Painting, an art he had set aside,
Becomes a form of meditation,
Each brushstroke a release,
Each color a new beginning.
The act of creation, once daunting,
Now feels like a dialogue with his soul,
A way to express what words cannot,
A testament to his evolving journey.

The Power of Presence

As he walks through the park, he begins
To appreciate the power of presence.
No longer lost in the depths of his mind,
He grounds himself in the here and now.
He watches the squirrels dart among the trees,
The way the sunlight filters through the leaves,
The subtle dance of shadows on the path.
These details, once overlooked,
Now fill him with a profound sense of connection.
He learns to appreciate the ordinary,
The routine, the seemingly mundane.

The simple act of sitting on a bench,
Watching the world unfold,
Becomes a meditative practice,
A celebration of existence.
Building New Routines
Routine becomes a cornerstone of his healing.
He establishes a morning ritual,
A time for reflection and gratitude.
He writes in a journal, recording thoughts,
Dreams, aspirations, and small victories.
Each entry is a testament to his journey,
A record of his transformation,
A reminder of how far he has come.
He begins to incorporate exercise into his days,
A gentle jog through the park,
The rhythmic sound of his feet on the pavement
A reminder of his body's strength,
Of the life that pulses through him.
These routines, though modest,
Provide structure and stability,
A counterbalance to the chaos of the past.
They anchor him in the present,
Allowing him to move forward with intention.
Embracing the Journey
He starts to embrace the journey,
Understanding that healing is not a destination
But a continuous process,

A series of steps, both small and large.
He acknowledges the setbacks,
The days when the shadows feel longer,
When the pain resurfaces with intensity.
These moments, though challenging,
Are part of the ebb and flow of life,
A natural progression toward healing.
He learns to navigate these fluctuations
With a newfound grace,
Recognizing that they do not negate his progress
But are integral to his growth.
In the park, he finds a new rhythm,
A balance between movement and stillness,
Between action and reflection.
Each day is an opportunity to practice,
To integrate the lessons learned,
To continue evolving.
The Strength of Community
He starts to engage more with the people
In his life and in the park.
He strikes up conversations with familiar faces,
Exchanging greetings, sharing stories.
The elderly man on the bench, once a distant figure,
Now becomes a companion of sorts,
Their nods and smiles a silent acknowledgment
Of shared experience and understanding.
He joins community events,

A local book club, a gardening group,
Finding solace in collective activities,
In the camaraderie of like-minded individuals.
These interactions, though small,
Reinforce his sense of belonging,
Of being part of something larger than himself.
They remind him that he is not alone
In his journey, that others share
In the pursuit of connection and renewal.
The Evolution of Hope
Hope, once a fragile glimmer,
Now evolves into a steady flame.
It illuminates his path,
Guiding him through the uncertainties of the future.
He no longer clings to hope
As a mere possibility but embraces it
As a driving force,
A source of strength and inspiration.
Each day, he witnesses the power
Of hope in action.
In the simple acts of kindness,
In the resilience of the human spirit,
In the beauty of the world around him.
He understands that hope
Is not a passive state but an active pursuit,
A commitment to finding joy
In the midst of struggle,

To seeking light in the darkness.
Looking Ahead with Optimism
As he gazes into the future,
He does so with a sense of optimism.
The path ahead is still uncertain,
Filled with both challenges and opportunities.
But he faces it with a renewed sense of purpose,
A willingness to embrace whatever comes his way.
He acknowledges that the future
Will bring its own set of trials,
But he is prepared to meet them with courage.
He envisions a life filled with possibility,
Where the past serves as a foundation
For future growth and exploration.
He dreams of new experiences,
Of meaningful connections,
Of a life that reflects his true self.
In each new dawn, he finds a promise,
A chance to live fully,
To continue evolving,
To embrace the journey with an open heart.
The Final Embrace
One evening, as the sun sets in a blaze of orange and red,
He takes a moment to reflect on his journey.
The road has been long and winding,
But it has led him to a place of peace.
He understands now that healing is a lifelong journey,

A series of steps, both forward and backward,
Each one a testament to his resilience.
As he stands by the edge of the park,
He feels a profound sense of gratitude.
For the lessons learned, the growth achieved,
For the strength found within himself.
He smiles to himself,
A quiet, contented smile,
And takes a deep breath.
He is ready for whatever comes next,
Embracing the future with hope and resolve.
In the twilight of the evening,
He sees the world with new eyes,
And for the first time in a long time,
He feels truly at peace.

9. The Dawn of Tomorrow

As dawn breaks with golden light,
He feels the warmth, so pure, so bright.
The night has passed, the day is here,
A future bright, devoid of fear.
The first rays touch his waking skin,
A gentle nudge to where he's been.
The darkness of his past now fades,
Replaced by the soft, inviting shades.
The sky stretches wide, a canvas new,
Painted in hues of every pastel view.
Clouds drift slowly, as if to say,
That each moment is a chance to sway.
He steps out into the morning's grace,
The world unfolds at a slower pace.
The air is crisp, the earth anew,
Every breath feels like a promise true.
With a smile that lights his face,
He feels the rhythm, finds his place.
The journey hard, the road was long,
But in his heart, there's now a song.

The melody of hope, so soft and sweet,
Plays gently with each step and beat.
The echoes of his struggle turn to peace,
A testament to how his pain's released.
The morning dew, the rustling leaves,
Whisper secrets of what he believes.
Every sound is a note in the song,
That guides him where he truly belongs.
He knows that life is ever-changing,
But with each change, a rearranging.
The pieces fall, the puzzle's clear,
That love and loss are both so dear.
Each moment past, though filled with strife,
Now adds a layer to the rich tapestry of life.
He sees the threads that weave his tale,
In hues of joy and shadow, both prevail.
The scars of yesterday have faded some,
But their lessons remain, they've not undone.
He carries them as part of his story,
Not as burdens, but as markers of glory.
He steps forward, head held high,
With dreams that reach up to the sky.
The boy who once was lost and cold,
Is now a man, with courage bold.
In every sunrise, a new hope found,
In every heartbeat, a strength unbound.
He feels the promise of each new day,

Guiding him in a gentle, encouraging way.
The dawn of tomorrow, a promise bright,
Guiding him through the darkest night.
Each step forward is a step towards light,
Into a future that feels so right.
He embraces the new, with hope so true,
A future filled with skies of blue.
Where once there was a fearsome void,
Now there's a vision, unmarred and unspoiled.
The journey has brought him to this place,
Where he finds strength and endless grace.
The battles fought have forged his soul,
And now, he moves towards a greater goal.
He pauses at the edge of a lake,
Where the morning's mirror seems to awake.
The stillness of the water reflects his face,
A quiet reminder of his own inner space.
The dawn's embrace, a warm and kind,
Welcomes him to a life redefined.
In the morning's glow, he starts anew,
With a heart that's brave and true.
The path he walks is soft and wide,
Beneath a sky where dreams reside.
He listens to the birds as they sing,
A symphony of hope that makes his heart swing.
The promise of tomorrow, now so clear,
Offers him a future without fear.

He feels the weight of yesterday lift,
Replaced by a calm, uplifting gift.
The days ahead are open, vast,
A canvas where his dreams are cast.
The shadows of the past no longer confine,
For he's embraced a light divine.
With each dawn, he feels the power,
Of a new beginning, hour by hour.
The whispers of the future call to him,
Guiding him through each horizon's rim.
He gazes at the horizon, wide and true,
Where the sky meets the sea's deep blue.
He imagines the possibilities that lie,
In the expanse of the open sky.
The dawn of tomorrow, a beacon bright,
Guides him towards a life of light.
With every step, he leaves behind,
The remnants of the past, intertwined.
He moves forward, with courage and grace,
Embracing the future he will face.
The dawn's promise is a gift so rare,
A testament to a life prepared.
In the light of this new day's crest,
He finds a quiet, comforting rest.
The shadows of his past now softly fade,
As he steps into a future unafraid.
Embracing the moments, both big and small,

He learns to cherish, to give his all.
The dawn of tomorrow, with its gentle glow,
Is a testament to how much he's grown.
As the day unfolds, he feels the shift,
The dawn's embrace is a precious gift.
He welcomes the future with open arms,
Free from the past's lingering harms.
The world is fresh, the day anew,
Filled with promise and skies of blue.
He walks forward with a heart renewed,
Embracing life with a hope imbued.
The dawn of tomorrow, a guiding light,
Shows him the way through the darkest night.
He steps into a future bright and clear,
With a spirit strong and a soul sincere.
In this new beginning, he finds his way,
Embracing the dawn of each new day.
With hope as his guide, he faces the morn,
In a world where new dreams are born.

10. Endless Eve

And now he stands at twilight's door,
A sentinel of light and dark, where shadows no longer roar.
The sky, a canvas brushed with hues of gold and deep indigo,
Weaves a tapestry of dreams where new hopes gently grow.
The dusk that once veiled him in its cold embrace,
Now whispers promises of a soft, warm place.
Where twilight's hues blend in a serene dance,
He finds solace in a delicate trance.
Each star that emerges in the velvet night,
Is a beacon guiding him to a future bright.
Their twinkling eyes, ancient and wise,
Hold secrets of joy beneath the midnight skies.
The moon, a silent guardian in its silver shroud,
Bows to the night with a grace so proud.
It bathes the earth in a silvery gleam,
A reminder that even shadows hold a dream.
The night breeze, like a gentle whisper,
Carries tales of hope as it drifts and shivers.
It speaks of dreams where sorrows ease,
And in its caress, he finds sweet peace.
In this moment, where day and night converge,
He feels the pulse of life begin to surge.

The endless eve, a canvas vast and grand,
Wraps him in its soothing, velvet hand.
The evening stars, a silent choir in the sky,
Sing a lullaby to the world below, and to him, a gentle sigh.
They dance in rhythm with the night's soft tune,
A celestial waltz beneath the silver moon.
He knows that life will rise and fall,
Like the tides that kiss the shore, then call.
Yet through it all, he stands tall,
In twilight's embrace, he hears the call.
The night, a painter with a palette rich,
Spreads colors across the sky, each hue a stitch.
In the fabric of his soul, these colors blend,
Creating a masterpiece that knows no end.
For in the eve where shadows softly play,
He's found the strength to greet the day.
The endless eve, no longer a darkened stage,
Is now a canvas where joy writes its page.
The evening breeze, a gentle hand,
Lifts him up to a promised land.
It carries whispers of a world reborn,
Where past sorrows are gently worn.
The twilight sky, once a shroud of despair,
Is now a stage where dreams declare.
Every star a note in a symphony,
Each one adding to his harmony.
He steps forward with a heart unbound,

Where happiness and hope are eternally found.
The night sky, a vast expanse of grace,
Welcomes him to a life he can now embrace.
He's learned that even in the night's embrace,
There's a boundless space where dreams can race.
So as the sun dips below the horizon's crest,
He smiles, for he has found his rest.
The night, a vast and silent sea,
Is no longer a place of misery.
It hums a lullaby of peace and grace,
Inviting him to a tranquil space.
In the endless eve, where dreams reside,
He walks with hope as his guide.
The night is long, but dawn draws near,
And in his soul, there's no more fear.
The stars, like silent witnesses to his tale,
Sparkle with a light that will never pale.
They celebrate his journey, each one a gem,
Reflecting the joy that shines within him.
He embraces the eve with a heart renewed,
Where happiness and hope are subtly fused.
The twilight sky, a canvas of endless grace,
Welcomes him to a life he can now embrace.
The darkness, once an overwhelming cloak,
Is now a veil that softly strokes.
It wraps him in its gentle guise,
A tender shroud beneath the starlit skies.

With each step into the twilight's embrace,
He finds a rhythm, a gentle pace.
The night, no longer a heavy shroud,
Is a soft cloak of dreams unbowed.
The twilight, a bridge between day and night,
Holds the promise of future's light.
As the world sleeps beneath the celestial dome,
He steps into the eve, no longer alone.
In the endless eve, he finds his place,
Where every shadow is touched by grace.
The night, a realm of beauty and calm,
Offers him a gentle, healing balm.
As the hours stretch and the stars gleam bright,
He savors the serenity of the night.
The endless eve, a time of reflection and peace,
Offers him a moment where sorrows cease.
And as he walks beneath the starlit sky,
He feels the whispers of a gentle sigh.
The night, once an endless expanse of fear,
Is now a haven where happiness draws near.
The dawn of tomorrow, a promise true,
Shines on the horizon, a golden hue.
In the endless eve, he's found his song,
A melody of hope that will carry him along.
The night, a canvas of endless dreams,
Glows with a light that gently beams.
It cradles him in its soft embrace,

Guiding him to a future full of grace.
And with each twilight, each gentle night,
He finds a new path bathed in light.
The endless eve, where dreams are spun,
Is the dawn of a new life, begun.
He steps into the twilight's embrace,
with a heart that's found its pace.
Yet as he treads this tranquil land,
A shiver weaves through twilight's strand.
The eve's warmth seems to wane and drift,
Replaced by a chill, a subtle rift.
In the distance, a light softly dances,
A fleeting glow, as if fate glances.
It flickers like a star's distant gleam,
Or a lantern from a forgotten dream.
He strides toward the spectral hue,
But the light retreats, a ghostly view.
Shadows stretch and whisper low,
An eerie murmur, an unbidden foe.
A voice upon the night's cool breath,
Softly speaks of fear and death.
Though words are lost, the tone is clear,
A hint of dread, a call sincere.
The warmth of the eve grows cold and thin,
As he senses a presence, a hidden sin.
With a heart still brimming with hope's embrace,
He turns away from the enigmatic space.

But the light has vanished, the voice withdrawn,
Leaving him in twilight's mystic dawn.
The dawn is near, yet shadows play,
Hints of mystery in the coming day.
In this endless eve, the journey's quest,
Leaves him pondering what comes next.
With courage firm, he meets the night,
But shadows whisper of the coming light.

www.ingramcontent.com/pod-product-compliance
Lightning Source LLC
Chambersburg PA
CBHW021548150726
47990CB00006B/2448